The Ninth Child

A Nazi Mayor's Jewish Son

[Nasjonal Samling or National Unity was a fascist party in Norway from 1933 to 1945]

FRANK ROSSAVIK

Order this book online at www.trafford.com
or email orders@trafford.com

Most Trafford titles are also available at major online book retailers.

Printed in the United States of America.

ISBN: 978-1-4907-4915-0 (sc)
ISBN: 978-1-4907-4916-7 (hc)
ISBN: 978-1-4907-4917-4 (e)

Library of Congress Control Number: 2014918318

Trafford rev. 10/10/2014

www.trafford.com

North America & international
toll-free: 1 888 232 4444 (USA & Canada)
fax: 812 355 4082

Foreword

Anyone who survived the Second World War has a history to tell. Sometimes one can get the impression that all of these stories are available in book form. Therefore, I was skeptical when Spartacus Publishing asked if I would like to find out and describe the history of Edgar Brichta (b. 1930), a Jew from Bratislava who came to Norway in 1939. Are still more books really needed about right and wrong, as well as victims, heroes and villains in this sad chapter in the history of the world?

But when I read a paper prepared by historian Bjarte Bruland, based on his initial research and discussions with Edgar, it stirred my interest. This is a different war story.

Part of the strength of it, I think, is that things that are often seen as bordering on caricature, and often with good reason, in this instance are less clear. Edgar is undoubtedly one of war's victims. He lost his family. But while the war lasted, he was an adventuresome child who had fun, even along with German soldiers. Edgar remembers a lot of what happened with and around him. He did not understand the drama and urgency until later. As he himself says: "For me the war was like living in a book by James Fenimore Cooper." This author is best known for 'The Last of the Mohicans'. Many of the people who more or less randomly appeared to help Edgar to escape the Nazis, are also complex. The bad guys are not quite black, and the heroes are not all white. This makes a story more interesting. At several critical points in Edgar's life are things that are difficult to explain. One can almost believe that he had his own guardian angel, although he is not religious.

Thanks to Edgar Brichta for making his records available, telling me his story through long interviews over four days; responding to supplementary amounts of e-mails, and writing his own epilogue. This was demanding of an elderly man, although he is in good shape. Thanks also to everyone else who showed up despite somewhat advanced age, and with a not groundless skepticism toward journalists. Thanks to Bjarte Bruland of the Jewish Museum in Oslo. He wrote the note which gave me a firm foundation for further work, and has also served as a constructive publishing consultant. Thanks to the editor-in-chief Frode Molven in Spartacus for a new, good cooperation. Thanks to the institution 'The Free Word' for funds. Thanks to my husband, the Czech Vojta Ježek, for good help with matters dealing with his country and Slovakia (and for much else!). Thanks to Arild Heggen in Nordfjordeid, for important help with the chapter that deals with Edgar's time there. Thanks to the State Archives in Bergen and the Bergen city archive, and Bergen Public Library, National Library, State Archives in Sogn and Fjordane and the HL-center in Oslo for good service. And ingratitude to the National Archives who refused me access to the court documents in the treason case of Arne Normann. These papers are generally kept confidential for 60 years. Although Normann's judgement date was older, the National Archive decided to use their ability to extend this period of confidentiality. It is one thing that the reasoning for this extension is threadbare, another of my complaints about the refusals lands in something that must approach a Norwegian record in bureaucratic tardiness. Finally so much time had been wasted that my appeal to the Department of Culture could not be resolved before my manuscript was due.

Fortunately, the problems could be overcome by using other written and oral sources. However despite a lot of good help, I stand of course solely responsible for any errors that may have crept into the text as it now appears.

Oslo, 10 February 2009

Frank Rossavik

Chapter 1

Laksevåg, a suburb of Bergen, late autumn 1942

With the benevolent assistance of the Norwegian police the deportation of Norwegian Jews to Adolf Hitler's death camps is in full swing. It knew nothing of Edgar Brichta. The Jewish refugee from Bratislava was out playing in Nygårdsvik. At a crossroad are two patrolling Wehrmacht soldiers. In halting English they ask for directions. Edgar has lived in the neighborhood for three years already, and responds eagerly-in German.

Trooper Gabauer from the Austrian capital of Vienna, became interested in the gentle, fair-haired local boy who spoke his language. And was he not familiar with the accent? The soldiers ask if Edgar will follow them. He is always ready for anything that seems exciting, and answers yes.

Later Gabauer invites him to visit the German garrison at Melkeplassen, and Edgar joins him. It turns out that they have much to talk about. Edgar comes from Bratislava, only five or six miles downstream on the Danube from Vienna. "We are almost neighbors", says the Austrian. Edgar's mother, Regina, comes from the German-speaking areas of Czechoslovakia, and her stepmother is from Vienna. Thus Edgar's German was a shade Austrian. Gabauer is happy for a little diversion - it's not as exciting just to occupy Bergen. Does he not ask any questions about how and why Edgar had come from Bratislava to Laksevåg? Maybe he does. Edgar cannot recall presently. Had Gabauer asked, Edgar would answer that he was sent on a holiday to Norway, and the tide of war makes it difficult to go home now. This is also what Edgar believes. Perhaps Gabauer was thinking simply that Edgar belongs to a German family who lives in West Norway for reasons that have nothing to do with the war. There were plenty of Germans in Pressburg, Bratislava's German name, and German families did live in the Bergen district before the war.

One evening they touched on scarcity of food. Edgar knows that his foster mother Agnes Normann is struggling to stretch ration coupons and any food supplements to feed her family. It turns out that the soldiers receive little good food. Gabauer wonders if Edgar has any idea if it is possible to buy more food. Edgar lights up: "I have some rabbits at home!" The soldier would like to have a couple. The next day finds two rabbits from the last litter on the road from the garden in Nygårdsvik to their fate in a German field kitchen at Melkeplassen.

Edgar happily tells of his business at home to his foster parents. Arne Normann gets upset and gives Edgar a scolding. He will have none of it. Arne is a prominent member of the National Union (NS) and appointed by the occupying power as mayor of Laksevåg. For him, Edgar is a risk factor. If it is reported that he hides a Jewish refugee in his home, he will have problems with NS leadership and Reichskommissar Josef Terboven. Especially now that the deportation of Norwegian Jews was in full swing. Edgar retaliates with "They are my rabbits and I will do with them what I want!" Arne is not pleased. Perhaps he became irritated by anti-Semitic inclinations also. Does not Edgar himself behave perhaps as a typical Jew, running a bustling trade whenever the opportunity arises? How did he and Agnes really get into this situation? What can they do with it now?

Max, Rea and Edgar Brichta in Bratislava on Edgar's 1st birthday. February 5, 1931.

Chapter 2

EDGAR BRICHTA'S FIRST FEELING of danger came when uniformed men came at night and knocked on the door of the apartment where the family lived in Český Těšín in the very north of Moravia in the then Czechoslovakia, on the border with Poland. His father was asked a series of questions, but Edgar did not know what the police wanted…or what they were looking for. Horror set in that night, but his father was able to explain away both this and later events. Before Edgar was born in 1930, Max (Maximilian) Brichta worked as a magician, hypnotist, violinist and sales representative. He also had been an officer in the cavalry of the Emperor of Austria-Hungary during the First World War. The author's portrait in a book he wrote about hypnosis, telepathy and psychic ability, tells also of a man with humor. If Max Brichta couldn't make his young son feel secure after the exposure to the gruff, uniformed men on the nightly visits, no one could.

Why the family in 1933 moved from Edgar's native Bratislava, capital of today's Slovakia, to the small town of Český Těšín, is not clear. But the most likely explanation for this is that in 1930 Max and Rea (Regina Brichta) together started a small paper and printing business at home in Bratislava. This did not support them, and they had to look for other opportunities. Český Těšín split by the river Olše into a Czech and a Polish part, was in an industrial area of great economic activity. It was also the head office of the large printing and publishing house Karel Prochaska. Since Max Brichta stated later on letterheads offering services to Prochaska on an agent basis, it seems that in 1933 he moved to Český Těšín to work for the company. 1933 was also the year when Adolf Hitler came to power in Germany. His National Socialist German Workers' Party (NS DAP) had since its inception in the early 1920's had a hatred for Jews, and animosity against the Versailles peace treaty declared after World War I. Although the Czechoslovak state under President Tomas Garrigue Masaryk, and much of the rest of the elite in the community were distinctly friendly towards the Jews, there had since the early 20's also been an anti-Semitic feeling in parts of the press and literature, as well as at the universities. It had its origins in Czechoslovakia's large German minority population, where many believed that the Jews took up too much space in the life of the society. So-called Volksdeutsche students had, among other things, organized an aggressive demonstration against Jewish students at the Komensky University in Bratislava in 1931. Shortly after Hitler took power in 1933, Andrej Hlinka, the founder of the Catholic- nationalist, or "fascist", Slovak People's Party (SNS), caused the celebration of the 1100th anniversary of Slovakia's first Christian church to degenerate into what the historian Livia Rothkirchen called a "wild demonstration against the government". "This and other nationalist manifestations were accompanied by anti-Semitic overtones in the Slovak press", she added.

It is the most likely rationalization after the fact, but still possible, that such conditions contributed to the Brichta family's decision to move from Bratislava to the more secluded Český Těšín in 1933. At this early stage, Adolf Hitler's power grab in Germany was not taken quite seriously by any significant number of people, but Max and Rea later showed that they were more than commonly attentive to the signs of the times.

From 1935 onwards the tension surrounding the Jewish situation in Czechoslovakia became noticeable to everyone. One reason for this was that after Hitler's seizure of power, the German government bid

Edgar, Rea and Edgar's grandma, Rosalia nee Haus. One of the men in the background is Max. Photograph is from around 1934.

welcome to the Jewish refugees from Nazi Germany and they streamed back in large numbers. With this came also the reactions.

Konrad Henlein's new Sudeten German's separatist party (SDP) had success in the elections in 1935, with 66 percent of the German vote and 15 percent of the combined population. Among the SDP were the leading paramilitary groups, which were particularly active after the party in 1937 clearly struck a pro Nazi course. Moreover, Hlinkaguard, the paramilitary organization of the SNS (Slovak National Party) 'nazi', also formed in 1937. This organization would soon start to harass Jews in Slovakia's cities. This did not happen, according to historians, until 1938.

Edgar remembers the uniformed men and the insecurity they clearly caused. It happened after 1935, the year his little sister was born. Several things indicate that the police raid on their Český Těšín home took place in 1937. It was carried out by members of the regular police on an ordinary assignment that did not have anything to do with the family's being Jewish. The uniformed men left a sinister feeling perhaps mixed with other emotions.

Mountain hotel Tatranska Polianka in the alpine Tatra landscape in northern Slovakia. Edgar and his mother visited the site together once, around 1934.

Not long after the raid, Edgar was brought by his parents to the larger city of Brno in Moravia, a part of today's Czech Republic. There he was placed in a Jewish widow's boarding home as the youngest member of the household. He also started for the first time attending a Jewish school. It is tempting to believe that the move was due to Edgar's family's feelings of uncertainty, but we cannot know for sure. After only six months in Brno, he was brought back to his parents' and Vera's new apartment in Bratislava. The family had moved maybe to be closer to relatives. Edgar had an aunt and uncle with their daughter living in Bratislava. A grandmother, widowed and in failing health, lived in her house in the Slovak city of Žilina

From 1937 onwards Edgar remembers more of what was happening around him. He resumed attending a general, non sectarian Slovak school. It lay some distance from where the family lived, but very close to his aunt Gizella, who was well off financially. She and her husband owned a three or four story house, where they lived on the top floor. Edgar liked to go there after school to enjoy leisure time for an hour or two. He suffered no distress at home; there was always enough food and adequate clothing provided by his parents, who now again ran a small print shop in the community. These visits with his aunt gave him a little taste of luxury. Early in 1939, Edgar with his parents and sister moved to Žilina where the family shared the apartment of his grandmother.

Edgar remembers glimpses of happiness in those years. He liked to go to school. Geography was his favorite subject. He had friends too, mostly Jewish. Edgar wanted a bicycle. This was more than his parents' budget allowed. Before Edgar's ninth birthday, his father went off to an auction, determined to get his son a two wheeler. He did not succeed. Instead, Max came home with a concertina, a hexagonal accordion with keys on both sides. In short order, he began to teach Edgar to play.

The family was a typical Central European one. Rea came from the southern part of Sudetenland, Czechoslovakia's German-speaking areas. Max was Hungarian by birth but became a citizen of Czechoslovakia when this nation was established after the end of WW1 in 1918. In addition to German his mother spoke Czech. His father was not fluent in the Slavic languages. But German was also the main language of the Austro-Hungarian empire. So German was the language at home when Edgar was born. The parents were aware of their Jewish identity. Neither one of them spoke Yiddish. They were not particularly religious, and they did not follow the Jewish food regulations. Sending Edgar to a general school was not a problem. Since both parents worked in the family business, they hired a babysitter for Edgar and Vera. Ludmila Rayova was a regular, local Catholic young woman. Some Sundays Edgar got to go with her to the church for Catholic mass. The song, decorations, candles and incense fascinated Edgar. The parents obviously knew about these church visits, but had no objections. The Christian Christmas was also highlighted in the Brichta household. Edgar remembers having Christmas trees, like other families on their street.

His parents made sure however that Edgar also had their identity under his skin. They took their son with them to the synagogue occasionally, and also paid a student to teach Edgar Jewish history. However, Edgar found out that this was not particularly interesting, so after a while the student suggested that he teach him chess instead. Thus, they mostly played chess in those hours, for the benefit of both.

Despite his parents' efforts to preserve normalcy and security, Edgar perceived an increasing uncertainty in their daily life. It did not take much. Reich Chancellor Adolf Hitler's appetite for more German territory had driven him to annex neighboring Austria in March 1938. Now he claimed Sudetenland in Czechoslovakia, mother Rea's homeland. Europe's other major powers did not object.

Sudeten Germans greeting the German invaders in October 1938.

They were more focused on preventing another major war. At a conference in Munich in the autumn of 1938, Great Britain and France agreed that Czechoslovakia's ethnically mixed border regions should be divided between Germany, Poland and Hungary. The Munich accord has become the very symbol of cynical and misguided appeasement. It was this paper Great Britain's Prime Minister Neville Chamberlain waved as he promised the world "Peace in our time".

With the agreement in hand, Germany now snatched Sudetenland in the west, Hungary marched into a Hungarian-speaking area in southern Slovakia, while Poland gained a small portion of the north. The justification of it all was that Adolf Hitler would henceforth calm down. This was not quite what Der Führer himself thought. Only a few weeks after the Munich agreement was signed, the Department of Foreign Affairs in Berlin convened to plan for what was to happen with what remained of Czechoslovakia. The Germans quickly decided to occupy Bohemia and Moravia, which comprised most of today's Czech Republic, and make it a protectorate. Hungary was given permission to annex a small area in the east. It is today a part of the Ukraine. Following this there only remained to decide what should happen to Slovakia. The solution was to make the country independent, but at Germany's mercy.

Already before the remainder of Czechoslovakia was butchered and fragmented, the Germans encouraged the formation of an autonomous Slovak government in Bratislava within the framework of the old state. Czechoslovakia showed weakened resistance after its first President Masaryk, retired, old and ill, in December 1935. He died in 1937. His close ally and successor, Eduard Beneš was forced out by the Germans. The new leader Emil Hacha buckled under German pressure and allowed Slovakia to establish an autonomous republic. Andrej Hlinka's successor in the Slovak People's Party, the Catholic priest Jozef Tiso, then became prime minister. Throughout the winter of 38/39 negotiations were conducted about the German conditions for the next step, the creation of Slovakia as an independent state. One of the most important conditions was that the Jews of Slovakia would be treated identically to Jews in Germany. Several meetings followed between Slovaks and Germans in Berlin and Bratislava. On the night of March 11, 1939 the German Foreign Ministry's envoy in Bratislava reported in a telegram home to the German capital that he had "alle Juden in der Hand" (all the Jews in hand). Four days later, the nation of Slovakia came into existence. At the same time, with Hacha's blessing, the Wehrmacht marched into Prague, which now became the capital of the German protectorate of Bohemia and Moravia.

There are limits to how much even determined parents can shield their own children from such events. Everything pointed toward a new war, and beyond this toward the disaster that would soon befall the Jews of Europe. The so-called Nuremberg Laws stated already in 1935 that all ethnic Jews were second-class citizens in Germany. This was the ideological starting point for the systematic persecution of Jews, even though it was a few years before all hell broke loose in earnest. Eager Austrians were the first with a major pogrom, persecution of Jews, in Vienna in March 1938. This took place just before the country was incorporated into Germany through the so-called Anschluss (union of Germany and Austria to create a 'Greater Germany'). Kristallnacht (Night of the Broken Glass) in Berlin the night of November 10, 1938 is remembered better. On that day, over a hundred Jews were killed, thousands arrested, synagogues burnt and many stores destroyed. The phenomenon spread quickly both in and outside Germany.

The Norwegian, Odd Nansen, with whose humanitarian organization the Brichta family would soon become familiar, visited Bratislava in early March 1939. Jozef Tiso was Prime Minister for an autonomous Slovakia but not yet president of the German puppet government that would soon follow. Nansen went there because of reports of persecution of the Jews under the auspices of the Hlinka-Guard. In the historical book 'Along the Road' Nansen tells among other things that he found a prison camp established in a Bratislava park where several hundred Jews were incarcerated under, putting it mildly, miserable conditions. Along the barbed wire, armed members of the Hlinka guard were patrolling. Upset, Nansen went to the private office of the organization's leader, Prime Minister Tiso, gained access and was received "with outstretched arms".

> He was a fat, squat clergyman in a floor-length cassock, with a golden holy cross dangling on his chest and with glaring black eyes behind gold-rimmed glasses.

Odd Nansen described what he had seen, and asked Jozef Tiso how something so unworthy could happen under his, a prominent clergyman's, leadership.

> I pointed to the golden cross which during my speaking jumped up and down on his fat abdomen because he constantly made the sign of the cross and rolled his eyes to show his great dismay.

Josef Tiso promised Nansen to investigate about the camp, about which he claimed not having had any prior knowledge. The Norwegian also went to see Bratislava's police chief on the same errand, and received the same assurances there. Odd Nansen then traveled to Vienna, where the most brutal persecution of Jews had started long ago - in full view. What he saw made such a tremendous impression on him that Nansen had barely calmed down when he wrote his book 30 years later. After a short time in Vienna he took the trip back to Bratislava again, to follow up with Jozef Tiso and his promises. In the time interval the priest had become the president of a formally independent state, and could not be reached. Nansen found that the detention camp he had discovered and complained about, had actually been dissolved, and the Jews released. In practice, the Jewish situation was not significantly improved because of it.

In the next few days, Nansen saw two synagogues burning. With his own eyes he could observe how the Hlinka Guard went out every evening to rob and beat up Jews, often with the assistance of Nazi hooligan groups who crossed the border from Austria.

How much the Brichta family experienced the unpleasantness of this phase is uncertain. Edgar remembers only two specific instances. One was when the family's radio equipment was confiscated. The other was when he went to school in Bratislava, he passed by a High School where groups of uniformed boys marched, banged on drums and chanted slogans. His mother warned him never to stare at them but just walk right by. Edgar remembers this as the Hitler Youth, but it most likely were 'Hlinkova Mladež, Hlinka Guard youths. Old film footage shows that it was not easy to tell the difference between them and HitlerYouth and that they must have seemed daunting to many.

Already at this time Edgar had an advantage as he was blond, blue-eyed and thus did not resemble the caricatures of Jews that Nazi newspaper continuously printed.

It was probably also in March 1939 Max and Rea Brichta decided it was time to move again. This time to Žilina, a Slovak city near the Polish border. It was where Max had been born in 1896. Grandmother Rosalia still lived in their old two story house. There, the family shared the grandmother's apartment. Edgar started at a Jewish school. This time there is no doubt that the move happened because of the increasing unpleasantness Jews experienced in Bratislava, and because Jozef Tiso's Catholic fascists had come to power. His parents must have thought that Žilina would be a quieter corner in what was becoming more of a Holocaust for Jews. At first it went fine in the new town.

Edgar and Vera together with parents in 1938.

Edgar was fond of animals, so his parents bought two chickens - "Pipkis" - for him. He could spend hours with them in the backyard, while the world went by.

Tiso's regime fulfilled its promise to Germany and went to work against the hated ethnic group. Edgar remembers signs with inscriptions that "Jews are not welcome" appearing more and more around the city. Also at home with mom and dad there was more talk about "us" and "them" for each day that passed.

It rapidly became much worse. Interestingly enough, the Slovak government was slightly more lenient towards "their" Jews than the Germans appreciated. Until Hitler-Germany's collapse in 1945 there was a tug of war between Bratislava and Berlin about how hard on the Jews they should be, says Raul Hilberg in the standard work "The Destruction of the European Jews". It included everything from expropriation of assets to Jews being deported to concentration camps. The new state's first "Jewish Legislation" from April 1939, functioned for example with a definition of where Jews were defined as only those who were religious, meaning those who were members of Jewish religious organizations, as well as Jews recently converted to Catholicism. If this law had prevailed, it could have helped the Brichta family. But this definition 'was much too flabby by German standards' as noted by Hilberg, and soon was made harsher.

Another struggle came later, when the Germans demanded that Slovakia pay for the transportation of Jews to the mass-extermination camps in Poland. The money was to come from confiscated Jewish property and -allegedly- was to cover the cost of transportation as well as maintenance, clothing and food in the camps. At the same time the Catholic Church requested that Jewish converts to Catholicism in Slovakia should not be deported. Other members of the Slovak regime wanted to exempt Jews who had married Catholics, as well as Jews who made important contributions to what was defined as key positions in their community. Germany and Slovakia eventually signed an agreement consisting of two conditions. One was that the selection of Jews for deportation should be made according to criteria that the Catholic Church could accept. The second condition was that Slovakia would pay 500 Reichsmark for each Jew who was sent. According to Raul Hilberg, the Germans gradually discovered that this as a whole led to Jews deported from Slovakia to extermination camps was not speedy and inclusive enough for their liking. At the negotiation the Slovaks were told "that in practice they could save money by exempting baptized Jews" as Hilberg writes. Annoyed Germans additionally suspected Italy of continually influencing the Slovaks. In his early political career, Jozef Tiso had become acquainted with his fascist colleague Benito Mussolini. Although Mussolini did bring Italy into alliance with Germany, he remained lukewarm to Adolf Hitler's persecution of Jews.

The Slovak regime had a radical, unconditionally Nazi friendly wing which wanted to get rid of all the country's Jews, and another more skeptical and moderate wing which wanted to retain some of the Jews. Even if Jozef Tiso belonged to the more moderate faction, in his perorations he revealed that he unquestionably was a Jew-hater. Regardless of his allegiances he was at the helm of a regime that managed to transport about 70,000 of the country's 90,000 Jews to death camps by the end of the Second World War. Tiso was also executed after the war - for treason.

The moving activities suggest that Max and Rea Brichta were more alert than most about what was happening around them, and less optimistic. It became increasingly difficult to maintain anything that could resemble a normal life. And - almost tragicomic - September 1, 1939, it turned out that they had moved right into the path of the German campaign against Poland. Jozef Tiso gave Hitler's soldiers safe passage through Slovakia. Now the German war machine roared through Žilina on their way to Poland. Grandma's house was located in a north corner of the main thoroughfare. Edgar sat by the window and watched the endless column of tanks, trucks, guns and soldiers, some on motorcycles. He could not believe there were so many vehicles in the world. Day and night hour after hour the Germans roared past, and the air was thick with exhaust. Edgar will remember the stink forever.

Now it was obvious to everyone that there was no way around a new major European war, and even Max Brichta couldn't talk reality away. Instead he took Edgar on his lap, and tried a new twist: Although this looked scary, there was really no reason for concern. As soon as the Germans came into Poland heavy rains would ensure that all the German tanks and guns would sink in the swampy terrain, he explained. And then Polish soldiers would take care of the Germans.

Somehow Edgar's parents became aware of the Norwegian Nansenhjelpen Organization, or *Nansen Help for the homeless, dispossessed and the stateless.* It was created in 1936 by Fridtjof Nansen's son Odd. Odd Nansen was at that time a newly qualified architect. He wanted the organization to honor the memory of his father, the polar explorer, who had conducted an extensive effort to help refugees, and others in need in Europe after the First World War. Fridtjof Nansen had also been the High Commissioner for Refugees under the League of Nations after WW1.

Nansenhjelpen became very active before and during WW2 helping especially political refugees from Germany. In April 1939 - after what Odd Nansen experienced at close quarters in Prague and Bratislava –' Nansenhjelpen' decided to bring Czechoslovak children of Jewish descent to Norway.

The desire to help refugees was not particularly strong in Norway at that time. Jews who tried to reach safety in the North in the late thirties were classified by the Norwegian authorities either as 'political refugees' or -more commonly - as 'racial refugees'. In Evian in France, in the summer of 1938 an international conference was held on how the wave of Jews fleeing from Germany and Austria should be addressed. Most countries, including Norway, rejected accepting Jews. Only the United States of America and some countries in South America showed a certain willingness to help. Some Jews still were granted entry to Norway, usually only for a temporary stay. In his report Odd Nansen acerbically writes that authorities demanded that refugees in no way should become a burden to the state. Even if admitted they could not get a work permit. There was unemployment in the country, and the unions wanted to prevent the refugees from displacing Norwegians. The unions made sure this did not happen by shutting all loopholes. In a book he wrote in 1970, Odd Nansen was still upset:

> What a pitiful and wretched legislative decree! - maintained in the midst of our law-abiding and advanced welfare society, whose foremost people did not hesitate to fill their mouths with liberty, equality and fraternity. Neither unions nor the governments can look back on that time without shame.

Thus, the refugees were left to make do with what alms the Nansenhjelpen managed to collect. It was anything but easy to get people and organizations to donate, says Nansen in "Along the Way". Some of the organizational donors even stipulated the money must not be used to help Jews.

In 1939 the Nansenhjelpen organization consequently had to struggle to obtain a hearing from the authorities for the children's rescue operation. The Minister of Justice, Trygve Lie, who later became the first UN Secretary-General, argued that "children without parents are much worse than children with parents". Lie's Director General, Carl Platou, wrote in a note that he, "like everyone in his government whose position demanded dealing with this problem", was very skeptical about granting residence permits in Norway for Jewish children. The danger of "being burnt jointly with them", as Platou wrote, was in fact large: "We must assume that the predominant number will remain in Norway and will become a Jewish element in the population and in businesses". Platou feared that this could arouse a burgeoning anti-Semitism, which he implied had obviously not affected him.

Finally, after long negotiations, the government agreed to grant permission for 40 children. The prerequisite for taking them was that they had not yet turned 10 years old, so it would make it easier, for them to learn the language and let them assimilate.

But there were already 16 Jewish children from Austria in Norway, and that turned out to be a problem. These 16 had been sponsored by a Jewish organization a few months after the *Anschluss*. The aim was to help children from Vienna with a vacation in Norway in 1938. During their stay in Norway, the situation of the Jews in Austria worsened. The sponsoring organization decided to let those children who wanted to extend their stay, remain. A more formal association, "Friends of the Viennese Children" was created under the leadership of the Jewish lawyer Leo Hersson. This organization asked for and received the Norwegian authority's permission for the children to stay in the Jewish children's home in Oslo. Originally 20 children arrived in Norway. Four were retrieved by their parents. Hence there were 16 Jewish children from Austria left in Oslo.

In 1939 the Ministry of Foreign Affairs requested that these 16 should be subtracted from the quota of 40 Jewish children from Czechoslovakia allocated to the Nansenhjelpen. The "Friends of the Viennese Children" protested, and received support from the Jewish Relief Society. The latter was formed as early as 1905 with the aim to support poor Jews in Norway. In 1938 the organization's goals and character were altered to concentrate on helping persecuted Jews from Germany.

Finally the Government relented. A report from the Nansenhjelpen leader in western Norway, Aslaug Blytt, states that "because of the difficulty at the Passport Office, the children's arrival was delayed and there were slightly fewer children than previously thought". Leader Blytt was referring to the Central Passport Office, responsible for immigration to this land. Some figures in the preceding paragraphs are subject to uncertainty, but the conclusion is clear: October 24, 1939 a transport with 37 Jewish children from Czechoslovakia arrived in Norway.

Thus the Nansenhjelpen action was a Norwegian afterthought to the far more extensive British "Kindertransport" organized by the Refugee Children Movement (RCM), which in 1938 and 1939 brought close to 10,000 mostly Jewish children to safety from Nazi Germany and its occupied territories to Britain. RCM ran out of money in August 1939, and stopped its activities. Also the U.S. accepted transports of children both before and during the war, but in a more modest number - about 1,400 Jewish children came across the Atlantic between 1934 and 1945. Both the British and American helpers had to struggle with their governments to take in children. A proposal to bring 20,000 Jewish children into the United States was defeated in Congress in February 1939.

One of those who traveled from Bratislava on October 24, 1939 was Berthold Grünfeld, who would later become one of the best-known psychiatrists in Norway. Another was Edgar Brichta. For Max and Rea, it was a welcome opportunity to get at least their son to safety. Norway, neutral during the first World War was expected to stay out of any new skirmish. Why did not little sister Vera also come with him is unknown, but the parents may have thought that she - who then was only four - would not tolerate separation from her parents. Edgar was nine, and much stronger. He could also be quite reckless and willful, and perhaps his parents were even more certain that he would do well without them.

Max and Rea Brichta likely feared that they would never see their son again. Yet to Edgar they presented the trip as a long vacation. They told him that he would get to see the ocean, which he had never seen, and that Norway was a beautiful country with high mountains, nice people and good opportunities for fishing. He would also learn a new language. Everything seemed very tempting for Edgar. When the day of departure approached, he and his mother went to Bratislava on October 21, 1939. There they went into a second hand bookstore, where Edgar got to choose two books for his journey. One was by Jules Verne and the other a nature book about giant worms in Tasmania. Monday morning October 23, 1939 Edgar and his mother went to the railroad station to meet the dozen other children and the two supervising Jewish ladies.

Edgar cannot recall the separation from his mother as traumatic. He was just going on a vacation. His mother kissed him and admonished him to act nice, be polite and do what the adults told him to do.

The most direct route to Norway would have been through Poland, but the condition of war prevented any entry to Poland. The next most facile route would have been by way of Prague. Because the Slovak part of the country was no longer integrated with the Protectorate of Bohemia-Moravia, the available alternative was the train for Vienna. The trip was short. In Vienna the travelling group changed to a train for Berlin There they joined the larger contingent, 24 children from Bohemia and Moravia who had started the trip from Prague.

The group of 24 children starting from Prague was led by Ms. Sigrid Helliesen Lund a member of the staff in the central office of Nansenhelpen in Oslo. Sharing the task was Ms. Marie Lous Mohr who also was active in the Nansenhjelpen organization. First they had to get from the Friedrichstrasse railroad station to the synagogue whose Rabbi had arranged for a meal at a local synagogue. The Rabbi led the group from the railroad station to the synagogue. After lunch they would trudge to the Anhalter Bahnhof from where the tour would continue north. At the time Jews were not allowed to use buses or streetcars in Germany's cities. Hence the children and their caretakers had to take their long walks.

In her autobiography Ms. Lund tells of her trip from Prague in October 1939. She was accompanied by Ms. Marie L. Lund, also an active member of the Nansenhjelpen organization. The first destination was Berlin on October 24, 1939.

As we were walking along the street, the Rabbi up front followed by four grownups, two Norwegian and two Jewish ladies from Czechoslovakia, and the 24 Jewish children from Prague, many

Berliners cursed us, some threw wads of paper. Some even spat in passing. I remember one of our girls coming up to me saying: "Is it the custom of people to spit on the street here in Berlin? We were never used to this at home in Czechoslovakia." I could not explain anything to her. I only said this might have been done accidentally.

Edgar does not remember this drama, only that they were told to walk without looking at peoples' eyes. Berthold Grünfeld gives a similar account in the book 'Afterthought - a Conversation' which he published together with Jahn Otto Johansen. Grünfeld emphasizes that the Czechoslovak travelers and their Norwegian care takers reached Berlin on a day when the Germans were exuberant over the defeat of Poland in three short weeks by Adolf Hitler's modern armed forces.

> B.G.: Yes, it seemed as if the Berliners were celebrating a victory. The city was full of cheering people. We were accompanied to the train station (...). I remember very well that we were told that we should not look at people. We should either look down in the street or fix our gaze on buildings, because our Jewish faces could aggrieve the German feeling of pride.
>
> J.O.J.: Was there really any reason why you should keep your faces hidden?
>
> B.G.: No, but our leaders were anxious. It was a numbing anxious feeling that touched us all.

In Sassnitz Edgar saw the ocean for the first time and opened his eyes wide. He absorbed the seagulls, salty smell and other impressions while the entourage waited for the ferry that would take them over to Trelleborg in Sweden. From there, the journey went straight to Oslo with a railroad train. Edgar does not remember anything from his first visit to the capital, other than that he thinks they got there late in the day. Berthold Grünfeld says that even if it was only the end of

October, there was frost at the East Railway Station, and snow in the streets outside. The winter of 1939-40 would be exceptionally cold in the east of Norway.

While the largest group including Grünfeld now were guided for temporary stays in an orphanage in the Oslo area, Edgar with eight other children and a Nansenhjelpen chaperone waited for the night train to Bergen. Edgar does not remember whether he reflected on his situation just after his arrival in Norway, but Grünfeld answers Johansen's question: "We still had fear in us. The omnipresent fear, that is my basic feeling from my earliest childhood. Always anxiety".

Edgar knew a touch of fear for sure, but he was of a different type than Grünfeld, and had had a less difficult childhood. He felt mostly excitement and adventure on the road over the mountains to the capital of Western Norway.

Chapter 3

THE OVERNIGHT TRAIN FROM Oslo rolled into the train station in Bergen at dawn on October 27. It rained as usual, and the darkness did not let up. In contrast, there were bright smiles to see on the platform. The six members of the Nansen Committee who helped the children in Bergen, with teacher Aslaug Blytt in the lead, welcomed the group from Oslo to Western Norway's capital. For months, the committee had raised money and had identified suitable foster parents. 50-60 had signed up after appeals in the press, but unfortunately there was now far fewer children than the Committee had originally hoped for. More the reason, of course, to make a good reception for those who did arrive. First of all the nine and their escorting ladies from the Oslo Nansenhjelpen had to get straight out of the station, turn right, and cross the street to Hotel Terminus. Awaiting there was breakfast, willing foster parents, and answers to many questions.

Also the press had to get its share. *Bergens Tidende* was on hand with both a journalist and a photographer. It became a lead story in the newspaper later that day. The five girls and four boys were photographed at the hotel. Among those in the picture is Edgar who looked the most skeptical. BT prints that thanks to the Nansenhjelpen, the nine would get good foster homes in Bergen for the next two-three years:

> The children were accompanied by Mrs. Dr.Abrahamsen (probably Lova Abrahamsen, (author's. note) They seemed to have had a good trip, were well dressed and equipped, but gravity was clearly marked on their faces, and it was not easy to get a smile to lighten them. Several of them have had to escape several times, and some of them apparently hovered in suspense about where their parents were and about what their own fate would be.

Bergens Tidende did not specifically state that the children were Jewish. Some things were probably better left unsaid, then as now.

Conservative *Bergen Aftenblad* wrote: "It was a, - what can one say to tell what it was like? A touching sight would cover it the best". The paper also highlights one of the boys in particular: "Edgar 9 years old. A shuttlecock of fate escaping hither and yonder. And now here. The newspaper's journalist would not be the only one to focus especially on the only fair haired one of the group from Czechoslovakia.

In the Hotel Terminus sat Agnes Normann and waited anxiously. She had long tried to have children with her husband, Arne, but they had not succeeded. When Nansen Council earlier that fall went to the newspapers and searched for willing foster parents for refugee children from Czechoslovakia, she took the matter up with him. They agreed to apply. After a few meetings with the Nansen Help local committee, who had asked several critical questions, they were approved as foster parents. And now the day had come. Agnes and Arne wanted preferably a girl. Nevertheless, Agnes' eyes focused on Edgar, the slender, light blonde and blue eyed boy from Bratislava. He was 1.26m (4ft 2in) according to the identification card issued soon by the office of the chief of police for the district of Hordaland.

In 1939 Edgar came to this house in Nygårdsvik. The motorcycle in the foreground is Arne's BMW.

Edgar was struck by new impressions those days. He does not remember much from his first meeting with Agnes. There could not be much of a conversation as Agnes knew little German.

There was some back and forth activity at the Hotel Terminus. The luggage was delayed. It would arrive a few days later. Forms had to be completed. Additional appointments had to be arranged. The local committee of Nansenhjelpen distributed new, warm clothing for the children with the assumption that some surely would not have winter wear from their homes. Ahead of time the Nansenhjelp committee had assigned to each child a committee member to be responsible by keeping in touch with each child and his or her foster parents to ascertain that all was going well. For Edgar's part this became the physician Bergljot Horne. They greeted one another and she explained to Edgar how and how often they would be in touch. Gradually the children with their foster parents left the hotel.

One boy returned to Oslo after only one week. Three of those children in Oslo, however, came to Bergen in December, while two of the original nine were sent home to Prague at their parents' request in April of 1941. All three that left Bergen died later in the extermination camps.

When Agnes finally got going with her new, temporary family member, she set a course straight toward Nøstet. Edgar attempted to orient himself and to remember the way back to the train station. The two walked along Lille Lungegårdsvann, past The National Scene, the theater building for live performances, and finally down Nøstet to where the ferry to Laksevåg was waiting at Sukkerhusbryggen. (Sugarhouse quay).

Not counting brief trips with his parents crossing the Danube river on a small ferry in Bratislava, the trip to Laksevåg was the nine year old boy's second ferry trip. It was a short distance compared to the one from Sassnitz to Trelleborg. Nevertheless it did cross salt water, a part of the ocean in Edgar's view.

From the pier in Laksevåg they went by bus on the short trip to Nygårdsvik. Finally they walked on narrow ways first down, then uphill to the house, a brown painted bungalow, situated on one of the highest points. There Edgar was greeted by Boris the Lapplander dog. Soon Arne Normann arrived home from his job at the Norwegian sheet metal rolling mill.

Arne Normann was from Stokmarknes in the Hadsel community in Nordland. For his college education he went south to Nordfjordeid in the county of Sogn og Fjordane to attend Eidsgymnas (college) privately run with public support. The school had a good reputation. In particular, it tempted talented youngsters from around the country because it offered a degree in two years in contrast to the traditional three year programs. Arne Normann attended the science division during the years 1926-1927. At the college in Nordfjordeid Arne met hisfuture wife the local girl Agnes Sætre, one and a half years older than him. She was attending the language division. After completing his college studies Arne went to Trondheim to attend Norway's

Technical University where he received his degree in mechanical engineering graduating with the highest grade in his class. He spent some time working as an engineer at a shipyard in Holland, then became yard engineer at a shipyard in Laksevåg, before transferring to the Norwegian sheet metal plant.

Agnes did not pass her graduating exam in 1928. The following year she did pass. Eventually married, Agnes and Arne settled in Laksevåg - today a part of Bergen.

Edgar felt welcome and safe. He got a nice room, just to the right of the entrance hall. Then came a room with closets, and next Agnes' and Arne's bedroom. On the left was the living room. At one end stood a stove that was used frequently in the winter. Next to the coke burning stove, was a snug warm place for Boris. He carried his blanket to this spot every evening. At the far end of the room were large windows. A dinner table and chairs for special occasions was near a corner with view of the forest and, closer, Agnes' flower garden. Everyday meals were served at a table in the kitchen.

To begin with Edgar spoke mostly with Arne, who knew German well. For a while Arne had worked at a shipyard in Holland, and from there he took trips across the border east to refresh his school German. Both Agnes and Arne began to speak Norwegian with Edgar from day one, and he quickly picked up the language. He also established a friendly relationship with his foster mother even though she was more soft spoken and introverted then her husband. After a few days, he finally got his suitcase. Edgar thought his foster parents looked at his clothes and shoes with critical eyes. He felt that they found their new family member had come from poor circumstances. Years later when he mentioned this to Agnes she was surprised and explained she and Arne had merely been curious but not condescending.

Boy Scout Squirrel Patrol. Edgar on left.

Edgar started attending Holen school, between Nygårdsvik and central Laksevåg. He was praised by teachers for being quick to acquire the new language. Soon he also got remarks for disorderly conduct. One of his specialties was to shoot paper wads at the necks of the teachers and classmates.In both the school and the Boy Scouts - as a member of the Squirrel Patrol - Edgar instantly made new friends. One of them, Arild Birkeli, remembers that the time he met Edgar the first time when he came slinking out of a little grove near the house where he lived. The Norwegian boys reacted first with dismay - this was their forest - but they quickly let Edgar get into their group. Andersen Forest, unofficially named after the owner, dominated the district. Only right up by the Normann's house was a lawn and some flower beds. Behind the building were berry bushes and more flowers. Otherwise the forest was wild and big enough that it was exciting for the boys to play there day in and day out. Interesting things one could also find, such as used condoms.

Among outside activities the boys often played lead-toss. Edgar got his lead from Arne who shaped it as a small, thick tortilla. The game was to aim the rounded lead plates at a line in the ground some distance away. The one that came nearest to the target line would win. The prize was usually cancelled postage stamps. Besides playing that, the boys played 'rooster fight'. It consisted of two equal numbered teams. Each boy hopping on one leg keeping the other leg bent and not touching the ground. The arms were held crossed over the chest. The two teams faced each other on an empty flat ground. At a signal each team started their one legged hopp boy aiming for a member of the opposing team esteemed to be surmountable while avoiding the ones deemed insurmountable. Any participant who lost his balance was out as soon as the lifted foot touched the ground. The 'surviving' participants

Agnes and Edgar with Lyderhorn in the background.
This time it had snowed also in Bergen.

who reached the opposing start line turned around and repeated their effort with the remaining opponents. This was done until one ing. Each victorious rooster remained. Edgar, often the smallest rooster, compensated for his lighter weight by being agile and resilient.

Everything was new to Edgar the first autumn and winter in Laksevåg. Much was happening, time flew by fast. Agnes felt she was too heavy and physically unfit. She would try sundry reducing diets and seldom went out to socialize. She no longer felt up to using her skis so she gave them to Edgar. Arne got him ski boots, adjusted the ski bindings and off Edgar went skiing in his first winter in Norway. With friends he went happily to Damsgård mountain and nearby Lyderhorn behind. That year it snowed even along the coast of western Norway. Edgar highly admired his friend, John Kvamme for his skill on the ski jump. For Edgar, who never attempted ski jumping, John Kvamme was as close to a Birger Ruud as he could get. Birger Ruud was Norway's world champion ski jumper that time.

Edgar must have repeated his old and still unfulfilled desire to get a bicycle. For Christmas in 1939 he received a gift from Agnes and Arne. The bike was blue and small enough to fit Edgar. The only brake was a hand brake that applied pressure on the front wheel tire. As there was no freewheel, Edgar could slow down by using his feet in reverse. This maneuver worked when he did not move forwards too fast. He was delighted. Even on Christmas Day, he wanted to learn to ride. Arne ran next to him for a period of intense cycling lessons. It was not long before Edgar found his balance. He was delighted and soon started exploring the environs, sometimes recklessly. Once he got in the way of a bus and was thrown off his cycle. He did not get hurt but the rear wheel of his cycle got a slightly distorted felly.

Further south in Europe, war was raging. Although most people still thought - or at least hoped - that the neutral Norway would stay clear. People listened to their radio following the news closely. Three months after Germany conducted the 'blitz' against Poland, the Soviet Union attacked Finland. Thus the Winter War was started. England and France would send off an expeditionary force to Norway and Sweden. This was to appear as aid for Finland, but the Anglo-French forces were denied transit. Sweden and Norway feared that these troops were aiming to occupy Sweden's iron ore fields to ascertain that this resource would not become available to the Germans. The Norwegian and Swedish governments did not want to provoke the Germans. The mood was anxious. Conjectures proliferated, but no consensus could be reached.

The Altmark incident in February 1940 increased tensions. Altmark was a German military support ship for a large German cruiser. The cruiser's task was to sinkBritish merchant ships in the South Atlantic. The Altmark had to set a crisscross course to avoid British Royal Air Force planes as well as British Royal Navy vessels. As it strove to reach a German port the Altmark set a crisscross course off the coast of Jæren, (on Norway's west coast). The Altmark was confronted by several British destroyers. When the Altmark sought refuge in the Jøssingfjord near Sokndal the British wanted to board, but were intercepted by two Norwegian gunboats which gave notice that the ship was being controlled by Norwegian authorities and was not transporting prisoners. The Norwegian neutrality guard had in fact inspected the ship, without detecting the English detainees. Would the Norwegian boats now shoot against the British? No. The British defied Norwegian orders, boarded, and freed 300 prisoners. Seven Germans were killed in the action. For the government of Nygaardsvold this incident was a doubly embarrassing affair. The British had violated Norwegian neutrality, but so did the Germans. No foreign power was permitted to carry prisoners of war on board in Norwegian territorial waters. Now both parties in the great war doubted Norway's neutrality, as well as its ability to enforce it. And they both feared that the other would strike first.

For the Germans, the Altmark affair greatly contributed to the drawing up of the plan for Operation Wasserübung (water exercise) - the invasion of Norway.

Edgar fit right into Laksevåg, enjoying the new life. He became mildly startled one of the first times he was showering after gymnastics at Holen school. Some of the other students noticed that he was circumcised. The episode did not create anxiety, but Edgar remembers it as a reminder that he was different from the others.

He told friends little about his past. But it was widely known in his group that he was one of the refugees from Czechoslovakia that had been thoroughly discussed in the media. Edgar was usually called

"Czechie". Some believe they also knew he was Jewish, but the rule parents advised during those times was that one should keep one's mouth shut and not ask questions at the wrong time. Did his friends have any opinion relative to the term *Jew*? One of them, Sigurd Frichsen, tells that if someone displayed himself as being different he might be asked "what is bothering you, you Jew?" They hardly had any feeling about the meaning but it must have originated somewhere. Willy Dahl, who did not know Edgar, remembers a time during the war when he was saying something derogatory about Jews at the dinner table at home, and got a firm overhauling by his father.

Edgar kept up somewhat with news from Europe, but cannot remember how much he reflected on what he heard - nor on his family's situation. Perhaps he repressed any thoughts that otherwise would have weighed him down. Shortly after arriving in Laksevåg, he sent his parents a letter about where and with whom he had landed, and that he was fine. Besides that, he conveyed his birthday wish. There was no opportunity to call. Although Arne Normann had a phone, his parents never had.

Not long after came the reply from Žilina, a long letter in German, dated 11.15.1939. His mother thanked him both for the letter and Christmas wishes, and as usual for mothers, she felt that the letter from her son was too short. She wanted to know if he already went to school, if he had friends, if he had learned some Norwegian, how he communicated with Agnes and Arne Normann - in German? - and so on.

> Please, write in detail about everything. You know that I'm interested in everything, everything you do and how it goes with you. I am very interested. So, write to me in detail about everything.

Rea Brichta reassured Edgar that his two Pipkis, chickens, hadn't been slaughtered. They lived in the best of health, and the black one had also laid her first egg.

And now that her son seemed to be in safety, his parents felt freer to tell more realistically about the situation in their home:

> Please, Edgar, be courteous and kind. Then all will go well for you. Think of how many thousands of children who have it bad here. Unfortunately, not everyone has had the opportunity to get out. You are a sensible boy, and it is lucky for you that you got out. This you must always keep in mind, and therefore you must always make sure that you give your dear foster parents nothing other than joy. Maybe, God willing, so can I and Vera travel out sometime. Now it is unfortunately impossible.

His father is not mentioned in the letter. Was he arrested at this time? But a short greeting from Vera, is added:

> Vera has often asked about you and is wondering when you are returning. She is now in kindergarten and has already learned many fine songs and poems.

Just days after this letter came a postcard with a picture of Vera and the two hens, and with yet another reminder that those in Žilina wished for speedy updates from Norway:

> We sit and think of you, when will you again write a nice letter for us?

In late November 1939, another postcard came from his mother in Žilina. This time she signed with "Mutti, Vera und Papa", so maybe he was home again. Rea Brichta was obviously anxious because she had not received a response from Laksevåg. Edgar cannot remember if he sent any letter in the interim. She asked urgently for a sign of life from both Edgar and his foster parents, and also to get answers to her questions. The tone was more stressed than the first letter. The mother was obviously worried that Edgar might have experienced some stress with Agnes and Arne Normann.

> Make sure you do not cause your foster parents any concerns. Behave well. I am very glad that you are out there, and I wish that Vera also were now in safe place. It would not have been good for you to be here now. We pray to God that it does not get worse.

At the end of 1939 the war had come to an end in Poland with Germany the victor, while France and Britain had declared war on Germany. It had not yet broken out seriously on the continent. Certainly the Winter War between Finland and the Soviet Union continued, and World War II's first naval battle was raging outside Uruguay, but both events were after all at some distance. The Tiso regime's persecution of Jews in Slovakia had not happened so far. But of course, Max and Rea Brichta saw clearly what happened to the Jews in Germany and the now included Austria, and also in what now was called the Protectorate of Bohemia and Moravia. They must have understood what might be in the making even for the three of them. How much nine year old Edgar in Laksevåg understood - in the relative orderly life still prevailing there - is hard to say. He does not remember that time well either. Letters from home must have kindled some thoughts.

Just after the new year 1940 came, yet another letter from Žilina. Rea Brichta thanked for the letter she in the meantime had received from Edgar and for the Christmas presents he wrote that he had sent, but that had not reached them. Rea Brichta wondered whether Edgar now was able to ski. Midways in her letter she switched from German to Slovakian, the reason seems obvious. Rea Brichta wondered if Edgar had any religious education, if he had Jewish friends, and what religion Agnes and Arne Normann might adhere to. Vera had again asked for when her brother was coming home, and mother repeated her assurances: He is far better off in Norway than he would have been at home'. Nevertheless, he had to write home more often!

Edgar's maternal grandmother, who lived in the Protectorate of Bohemia and Moravia, and was not overburdened with letters, wrote that Edgar's grandfather, her husband, had died. She would enjoy doubly some lines from her grandson in Norway.

Chapter 4

THEN THE WAR CAME to the presumed safe Norway. Edgar awoke about four o'clock in the morning of April 9, 1940 to the sound of rifle shots and thundering cannons. Looking out of his window he saw Norwegian soldiers with heather fastened to their helmets crawl on the ground and shooting towards Kvarven, the fort that was to protect the entrance to Bergen a bit farther out to sea from Laksevåg. The soldiers there had managed to fire a few shots at the German cruisers, *Köln* and *Königsberg*, and their supporting ships, but because of poor training and outdated weapons, they had to give up the fight as early as seven AM. Then people could also see both German and Norwegian soldiers go along Laksevåg towards Bergen. Edgar's comrade, the three years older Sigurd, remembers the Norwegian soldiers as ill-equipped and rather discouraged. One of them fired a rifle volley at random over his back as he went.

Only from the forts on the banks of the Oslofjord did the German warships meet any significant resistance. It was sufficient to enable the members of the Norwegian Government to escape to Hamar before the German invaders gained control of the capital, Oslo. Also in Kristiansand there were some confrontations on the ninth of April. In the cities of Arendal, Egersund, Stavanger, Trondheim and Narvik it went as it had in Bergen. - Germans met little or no resistance. From these coastal towns the inland campaign would start. Arne Normann was among those who kept his head clear in the hours that followed the attack. He had been conscripted in 1929 and served the obligatory time in the Norwegian army. He was given an honorable discharge and was registered as a non-combatant, yet he decided to volunteer to fight against the German invaders. But first he would bring his family to safety. Agnes and he packed what little they could carry with them. Edgar was told to get ready to go, and before noon of April 9 they climbed on to Arne's motorcycle. As usual, Edgar sat behind Arne, while Agnes sat in the sidecar with Boris on her lap. They drove out to Fyllingsdalen, where Arne knew a farmer who could provide shelter for a few days. After arriving Edgar began to explore the farm. Soon he found a place where someone had recently dug under a bush. The soil was still loose. With his hands Edgar dug some and soon found a well-wrapped handgun which he proudly brought to the adults. The farmer was not thrilled. He had just buried the gun to avoid having to give it up to the occupying power.

They were on the farm in Fyllingsdalen a few days to see how things developed. The government led by prime minister Nygaardsvold had fled from Oslo to Hamar, and later went on to Elverum. It left a power vacuum. The leader of the National Union party, Vidkun Quisling, attempted a military coup on the afternoon of April 9. This was annulled by the German occupying forces within five days. A few days later Josef Terboven was appointed as Reichskommissar. There was not much credible information to be had, but people exchanged what they had. Arne and the farmer agreed that they would fight against the invaders. Both decided to go to Voss where the Norwegian military forces of the West had their largest base. Rumors had it that the Germans had set up roadblocks at Nesttun, and that it was dangerous to try to go that route. Nevertheless they decided to go. To remain passive was not an acceptable alternative. Before Arne left to join up with the Norwegian forces he and Agnes decided, that Agnes, Edgar and Boris were going to Nordfjordeid to live with relatives of Agnes for a period.

Arne as a soldier in the Norwegian army around April 1929.

Settlement in Nordfjordeid municipality where Agnes had relatives. (Photo: Sogn og Fjordane county records.)

While Bergen naturally enough was one of the German's main goals, the small community of Nordfjordeid would probably not attract Hitler's 69th infantry division for some time, they must have thought.

Therefore it ought to be safer there. Most likely Agnes and Arne were primarily concerned about their Jewish foster son: Best to keep him as far as possible away from German soldiers.

Nordfjordeid is a village in the Eid municipality. The village nestled on the Nordfjord in the north of the Sogn and Fjordane county. Edgar and Agnes arrived there by the fjord vessel and were received by her brother Harald. The family was operating the steeped in tradition Yris hotel, in the center of the community, and a short walk from the pier. The two story wooden structure was built before metal nails were available. The wooden planks were fastened to the timber beams with wood dowels. There was much for Edgar and Boris to explore. The dog enjoyed new hunting grounds. Soon he killed a rat and got praise. Just after, flushed with the good response, he killed one of the pigeons belonging to Anna Sætre, youngest sister of Agnes and Harald. Boris was scolded, Edgar consoled him. Anna donated the dead pigeon, after cleaning and roasting it, to Edgar. Edgar in turn shared the morsel with Boris. Edgar was on the move from the beginning. He found a village dominated by the long Eidsgata with its beautiful wooden houses, and a vibrant local society.

Also in Nordfjordeid the people were obviously affected when the war reached Norway. At this point in time many men were mobilized to fight against the invading forces, mostly in Valdres. Some might also have suspected that it would not be long before the Germans announced their arrival locally. Nordfjordeid was best known for Eksersisplassen, a large military training ground founded sometime around 1650, that made it the nation's oldest. Although more and more of the military operations in western Norway were transferred to Voss, lesser military exercises still took place on Eksersisplassen until 1939. When the war came, a spontaneous national protection battalion was established in Nordfjordeid. A small number of German prisoners of war were interned in "The Place", as it was called, it is uncertain for how long. This village was an excellent place for the Germans to occupy, i.e. as a base for controlling Northwestern Norway.

On May 9th the Newspaper *Fjordabladet* announced in measured terms what probably was the first German vanguard in Eid on the preceding day:

A group of Germans came to Nordfjordeid yesterday morning. The drove in here, and looked about a while. Then they took a trip out to Selje. It is rumored they were looking for Englishmen. If so they travelled in vain. Early today they departed.

No skirmish between German and Norwegian soldiers occurred here. The Norwegian forces in southern Norway had capitulated on May 4th and the Germans assumed power. The occupiers seized all military authority. County administrators were to handle the regional civil administration. Any acts of sabotage, propaganda and other "hostile actions" could be punished with death.

Then the Germans came to Nordfjordeid in earnest on May 15. One can find various estimates for the size of the initial detachment. But it was one battalion of the 69th Infantry Division. German battalions during the Second World War were usually at about 800 soldiers, including officers. Heavy duty for a small western village where about 600 souls lived during the war. Margun Gjul told about the experience in *Sogeskrift for Eid (History of Eid) 2004-2005*:

I cannot remember what day we saw the ugly military vehicles driving down to occupy Eid, but it was probably sometime into May. We were afraid that somebody would be stupid enough to take up arms and get killed. Fortunately everything remained calm.

A large number of military trucks drove in, with soldiers standing on the truck beds. Ove Sunde said that the road to Eksersisplassen went past Yris hotel where there was a sharp turn. Several of the cars went at high speed into the turn with the result that some soldiers standing at the rear end of the platforms tumbled out. The one landing on the bottom had to be looked after by a first aid detail. Another cried "Mutti! Mutti!" It certainly made an impression on young Ove, to hear a representative of the world's most feared army call for his mother.

A photo taken on the same day, or more likely a day or two later, shows the Germans marching in a parade through Eidsgata. Instead of guns, the Germans had binoculars hanging around their necks. The weapons were in trucks following the procession. Obviously the local inhabitants were to be treated with gentleness. The paucity of any accounts suggests that the Germans succeeded. No physical abuse ever was perpetrated on the local populace. Beyond practice target shooting there were never any shots fired. Margun Gjul:

The German soldiers were always very proper and disciplined. When they marched on the roads, they sang very nicely, and they also had a band with them.

Edgar has no clear memory of the day the Germans came to Nordfjordeid. Maybe Agnes kept him away. She was apprehensive as she had wanted to bring Edgar to a safer location than Laksevåg,

Marching German troops were included in a parade through Eidsgata in May 1940. (Photo: Sogn og Fjordane county records.)

German barracks in Nordfjordeid against Hola [town ~3miles west of Nordfjordeid]. Photo taken in 1954.

now maybe it might turn into the opposite. Edgar remembers that on one occasion he did see a major German parade marching through Eidsgata. It may have been the parade that was photographed, but the boy standing by himself on the right side of the street is probably not Edgar.

The Germans built a whole barrack town which at times housed up to 1,000 soldiers. All the new activity was obviously exciting for Edgar. For him the war, especially in the early stages, was pure adventure. The Germans planted trees and built barracks on Eksersisplassen and they erected a new gate adorned with the German eagle. They also built bunkers around in the area. Later in the war Nordfjordeid also became the German command center for the defense against the so-called Måløy raid [from the town 12 miles west of Nordfjordeid] conducted by British forces with Norwegian participation.

Wherever the Germans stayed in Nordfjordeid, there were guards with German Shepherd dogs. At fixed times armed soldiers went patrolling two and two. One day Edgar met a couple of them. In English - or maybe fractured Norwegian - they asked for directions to a fish store. Edgar thought this was a good opportunity to make use of his mother tongue, so he replied in German. The soldiers were clearly amazed that a little boy in Nordfjordeid mastered German so well and first stared at him and then at each other. Maybe Edgar stood there and smiled. At least the Germans smiled, after some seconds hesitation, and let him guide them. Nothing was better than having a real, native interpreter. In those days, Nordfjordeid had two places where to buy fish. One could go to the pier and buy directly from the fishermen. Many Germans did that and then they bought mostly eels. But the Germans led by Edgar chose otherwise. He went to Fiskebuda,

Boris and Kjukken (Fatso) in Nordfjordeid.

the fish market. It was run by a fellow named Lillestøl. Here, they chose a huge halibut. Edgar - who had never seen such a creature before - translated and negotiated on behalf of the Germans. Already in the days of April there were shortages and rationing of certain goods in Norway, especially flour, sugar and coffee, but there were enough fish in Nordfjordeid.

Back home, Edgar told about the exciting things that had happened that day and with particular emphasis on his new knowledge of halibut. Edgar remembers that neither Agnes nor Harald reacted negatively to his contact with Germans. It may seem incomprehensible.

Certainly Edgar may not have had much to fear in this phase of the war. This was long before Vidkun Quisling and the National Front took charge of the government and initiated the persecution of Jews in Norway. German soldiers abroad had not been commissioned to track down Jews. But one could never know what an officer could invent. If nothing else, he could report Edgar to the new police authorities. Moreover, one would think that Agnes and Harald feared for the family's reputation. Helping the occupation forces beyond showing a minimum of courtesy, could mean social suicide during the war. But collaboration became first and foremost an onus during the later stages of the war, when it became clear that the Germans would lose. In the early years many looked pragmatically at the occupier. Anyway Edgar received no warnings.

Happy and satisfied, he maintained contact with the Germans, was familiar with several, and continued his interpreting activity. Eventually, he became almost a mascot for the Germans in Nordfjordeid. They invited him to quarters, and there was much to see. Among other things,

Edgar observed farrier soldiers shoeing the officers' horses. One evening, he was also invited to watch a German film. Edgar cannot remember what it was about, only that Zarah Leander was in it. The Swedish singer and actress was one of the biggest at this time, especially popular in Germany and Austria. The Sætre family where Edgar was staying received routine reports of his adventures. When he told about the movie, Harald became angry. Maybe he felt that was too much of a good thing.

The highlight of the contact with the Germans came when a soldier took him up the mountainside to Myklebust dairy, the old firing range. One friendly soldier asked Edgar if he would like to fire a machine gun. The soldier aimed the weapon at the target and showed Edgar how to pull a trigger handle. A thrilling experience even if he did not hit the target. A Sergeant saw the underage 'assistant soldier'.

The real soldier got a severe reprimand while Edgar was told to stay away from the shooting range.

Was he afraid? No. Only once was Edgar scared while he was in Nordfjordeid. This was when one day he stepped on what looked like firm earth next to the barn. He sank hip deep into a manure pit before turning around and reaching firm ground. Even after a long bath, the stench of manure from cows, horses and pigs stayed with him for days.

Chapter 5

ARNE NORMANN PARTICIPATED IN what little there was of active war in Voss until the official armed struggle in South Norway ceased on May 4. He served at first as a guard at the munitions storage depot. Later he served at a machine gun post. Norwegian and German soldiers saw combat in Voss, but it is unclear whether Arne was directly involved. After the place was lost and the capitulation was a fact, he went home to Laksevåg. There he resumed his work as an engineer at the Norwegian Metal Plate Rolling plant. In June Agnes, Edgar and Boris came back from Nordfjordeid. Arne Normann was disillusioned by how little the Norwegian forces had been able to resist the German invasion. He found even more discouraging how little the British forces who were put ashore at Åndalsnes had accomplished. As he perceived it they were feckless.

Edgar remembers his foster father later made several derogatory comments about the British. He felt they used Norwegian troops only to cover the retreat of the British. He scoffed over the British brigade that came to Åndalsnes April 18 and evacuated two weeks later.

In August 1940 Arne Normann announced that he had joined the National Union, and soon after also the Hirden, NS ' paramilitary organization. The latter was mandatory for NS members. Why did Arne enter into this small Norwegian fascist party that had never managed to get wind in its sails, and now played on the same team as the occupier? Although his language skills and several visits to the country might have predisposed Arne to view Germany with a positive inclination, he had undoubtedly conceived the invasion on April 9 as an assault. Otherwise he would not have volunteered at the front. He had been a noncombatant with no obligation to enter active military service. His disappointment at the tide of war - and especially by what he saw as Britain's evasive movement - must have made him more susceptible to the National Unity leader Vidkun Quisling's propaganda now spread with renewed force. Edgar does not remember Arne showing Quisling nor NS any interest before the war. After the occupation Edgar found himself several times within hearing of the radio apparatus when the NS-leader was making exhortations for national unity(NS) and for cooperation with Germany in the fight against Bolshevism. Arne devoured the NS newspaper 'Free People', and all its propaganda *against* the Jews, the Allies and the deposed government of Johan Nygaardsvold ("the Marxist government"), and in favor of "the German defensive power".

Edgar also remembers that Arne Normann was a faithful reader of Knut Hamsun, perhaps partly because the famous writer had grown up on Hamarøy, not far from Arne's hometown Stokmarknes. Hamsun supported Germany and Adolf Hitler to the very end.

That in the summer of 1940 Germany appeared to be winning the war just by a walk over probably played a role. After taking Denmark and Norway, Adolf Hitler attacked Belgium, the Netherlands and superpower France. Contrary to all expectations, the French armed forces fell apart in a short time. Not until September one month after Arne became a member of Vidkun Quisling's party did Adolf Hitler first meet appreciable resistance - in the Battle of Great Britain.

In the autumn of 1940 there were many who thought that perhaps it was best to abide by what appeared as the new reality. Early during the war, Norway was full of people awaiting developments before deciding to join either the NS or the underground resistance movement.

Was Arne an anti-Semite, a Jew hater? It is impossible to say whether he was before the war. On the whole, there is no information about his political views then, to the extent that he had any. But the fact that he adopted a Jewish foster son in 1939, suggests that he may not have had any negative view of Jews. One can probably assume that it was Agnes' project to take the opportunity of getting one of the Jewish refugee children, and Arne willingly acquiesced. Agnes never became a member of the National Unity party.

When Arne Normann became a NS-man, he became exposed to negative views of Jews. Edgar remembers when from his time in Nygårdsvik Arne invited a handful of male Nazi members to a dinner meeting. After the meal the discussion continued around the table at one end of the elongated living room. Agnes, Edgar and Boris were by the coke burning oven at the other end of the room. One of the participating men stated that Jews were usurpers who enriched themselves at the expense of others. Edgar does not remember Arne's response on that occasion. Did not Arne also realize how absurd the situation was?

One day Edgar found a book on the coffee table in Nygårdsvik. It was a novel, and Edgar remembers the word "Jew" or "Jewish" in the title. It was about two stowaways who were discovered by the crew of a ship bound for America. Both were sent to the ship's brig. They also had to work washing dishes. One was Jewish. When this news reached the passengers a few of the ship's well off Jewish passengers, decided to bail out the Jewish stowaway and furnish him with a ticket for the journey. Thus the Jew enjoyed his trip to New York, along with his benefactors, while the other stowaway languished in a dark room far below deck. Edgar took in what was on the first pages of the book, but after a day the book was gone.

Laksevåg was then one of the 'reddest' municipalities. The well-liked mayor at the outbreak of war, Alf Pettersen, was a Communist. NS, founded in 1933, was very weak in the municipality. Membership was never much more than a hundred. Thus it became easy for a

Nazi party member to advance his career by attending meetings and expressing a willingness to serve under the German dominated government. After joining the Nazi party Arne Normann was rapidly designated as a local team leader, but it is uncertain whether this led to much activity at first.

The news that Arne Normann was a Nazi spread quickly throughout Laksevåg, and many were amazed. No one had imagined that he could have such tendencies. One place where "amazed" was too weak a word, was at Nansenhjelpen's local children's committee.

Until then, Edgar had only sporadically been in contact with Bergljot Horne. Once, Edgar had been with her at an event along with the other children who had come to the Bergen area from Bratislava and Prague. This was the only time Edgar met some of them since their journey to Norway. The reason is probably that it was safest for the children to live mostly anonymous and integrated into their Norwegian foster families.

When Arne Normann was appointed to be mayor and thus one of the NS' top men in the district, it must have caused quite a stir. The Committee was reconvened. Would not just Edgar, but also the other children be in danger? The Nansen people decided not to upset the 10-year-old, but they quickly asked for a meeting with Agnes Normann. In a report Aslaug Blytt wrote after the war, this was the situation:

> In the autumn of 1940 Edgar's foster father had become a member of the "National Unity" (NS party). Mrs. Normann was not a member of the NS and guaranteed that the man's membership had no effect on his relationship with Edgar, and that the boy would not be subjected to the Nazi influence.

The Nansen Council people were still obviously not completely reassured by Agnes' assurances about her husband. "Attempts to find new foster parents failed", was their added note.

Edgar remembers Arne told at home about his NS membership, and he knew very well what kind of party it was. Soon there was also NS-propaganda here and there in the house. But even then he felt no particular concern. Edgar thought that this was not really related to him, since he was just a child. War and other policies were for adults. The only thing Edgar remembers is that friends in Nygårdsvik were more reserved towards him, but it passed over quickly. The friends said that although they quickly learned about Arne's NS membership, Edgar was still seen as a refugee and should be helped. That he now lived in a NS- home was seen as odd, but nothing more than that.

An important reason why Edgar was never shunned is probably that Agnes was well liked in Nygårdsvik. She was introverted, but always friendly, and it was widely known that she was not a member of the National Unity Party This latter information people could hardly obtain from anyone other than Agnes herself. In as much as she made her non- membership status known, it was easy to interpret this as her distancing herself from her husband's choice. Her adoptive daughter Anne, who would come into the family in 1942, remembers that Agnes many years after the war said that she had been very much opposed when Arne joined the National Unity party. Agnes also said that one of her women friends who had joined the NS came to visit in Nygårdsvik carrying NS membership recruitment brochures. Agnes turned her away with the message: "If you keep up with this, you'll not be my friend anymore", as reported by Anne.

Edgar did not catch any of this, but he has one specific memory from the first autumn of the war: Arne Normann decided to add a bomb shelter to the basement for the family. Two workers were hired to take care of the matter. Part of the job consisted of blowing up a knoll on the north side of the house. Edgar naturally became excited when the two placed mats over dynamite that had been placed in holes drilled into the rock. Then one worker lit the fuse and ran for cover.

Reichskommisar Josef Terboven had installed his commissioners as ministers in Oslo, and now the local level of government stood in line.

Sitting mayors and municipal councils were deposed through a decree at the end of 1940 to be made effective from January 1, 1941. In their place would be appointed new mayors with absolute power, with an advisory body to be used only as needed.

Popular Alf Pettersen had initially continued as mayor of Laksevåg municipality after the German invasion, although the Communist Party was banned in August 1940. Later the Germans even offered him a ceremonial position of Oberbürgermeister, (honorary-mayor) which he declined. In the late winter of 1941 he had to step down because the National Unity (NS) had struggled persistently to get control of the local administration. They could not tolerate a Communist in such a position, according to Kjell Fossen in the *History of Laksevåg.* First they tried to get a representative from the old Citizens Parties to take on the position. This was the strategy in many communities, especially where there were no obviously qualified NS people. The occupying power and their helpful friends in the NS wanted to ensure that events would slide along smoothly. However attempts to find such a solution in Laksevåg did not succeed.

After some time Arne Normann came to be considered. He lacked both organizational and political experience, but he was a NS member, had no bad reputation locally, and was also an engineer - at the time a highly respected profession. Arne consented, after first having declined. Later during the occupation, he was appointed as director of the streetcar system in Bergen, which he later described as a promotion.

His foster father's lightning career in the NS changed the course of Edgar's position among his friends. As mayor, if not already as an ordinary party member, Arne Normann had become a threat to most of the people in Laksevåg. Edgar noticed the shift. Friends didn't shut him out, but were clearly more reserved. He noticed this also in the Holen School. There was no bullying, but still. Also for the teachers, it must have been hard to deal with a student who was now both a Jewish refugee and a kind of NS-child.

As the scarcity of food - and rationing - took hold, people started to augment their food supply using some methods that were legal, others not. Among the latter belonged the 'villa pigs'. A piglet could be bought on the black market, transported clandestinely to a hide-away pen in a yard or an orchard there to be fed and kept from making noise. Neighbors helped by donating food waste. In return they received a portion of the meat when the pig was eventually slaughtered. Once the family of one of Edgar's pals had one such villa-pig, and the boys made the rounds to participating households to collect food scraps. Once when Edgar and Willy with a barrel on a wheelbarrow went colleting scraps for the piglet, on a narrow road they met with a column of Russian prisoners of war escorted by German soldiers. The boys stood aside against a dense hedge. The German guards did not seem vigilant. As the Russian prisoners in ragged uniforms and worn out boots walked past, some of the ones passing closest stuck a hand into the slop barrel and put the slop in their pockets. The parents of Willy became apprehensive and asked Willy not to risk taking Edgar along on these slop gathering trips. On one occasion, he went to Agnes to complain that the others were so suspicious. He felt excluded because Arne was the NS mayor. Agnes said that "Arne is doing what he thinks is right". In her conversations with Edgar, he noted that she never expressed any disagreement with Arne.

For Edgar, life was now tougher, not only because friends behaved differently. The fall and winter of 1940-41 was also much darker than usual. Street lights were off at night. Occupying authorities ordered blackout curtains in all windows. Light bulbs had to be painted so they gave up minimal light. The intention was to make it difficult for Allied aircraft to orient themselves on their missions. Everywhere were gray clad German soldiers guarding. In the evenings there were curfews. Edgar really only thought it was exciting. He often ran out anyway. Once he got caught in the beam of a German soldier's flashlight in his eyes, but he did keep going out. Perhaps soldiers were more lenient with children.

One evening Arne Normann held an informal meeting with other NS-folks at home in the living room. The men sat by the window, while

Agnes and Edgar sat by the fire at the opposite end of the room. Agnes knitted or mended clothes, as she so often did. Edgar was reading but also listening to the conversation. One of the visitors came with powerful words against the Jews, claiming that the war was their fault. Edgar got a fright, but he believed that his parents could never be blamed for starting a war. The reaction of Arne was not to reply to this man. Edgar also remembers that the name Jonas Lie was mentioned several times in the conversation. Lie was the Nazi police minister during the war, later becoming head of the SS in Norway. Fortunately Edgar said nothing this time, but this was one of the few times he felt discomfort directly in his home in Nygårdsvik.

Edgar and Agnes' contact with his parents back home in Slovakia continued through 1940. Granted, only one letter from that year was saved in Edgar's papers, except that which came in January, and this one was from the end of November. But in it, Rea Brichta wrote she was sad that she had heard nothing "for weeks". As nothing arrived, they may have thought that Edgar was no longer in Nygårdsvik. But it was obviously Agnes took charge. Edgar had, according to his mother, not answered several of her recent letters. But in this period she was fairly accurate there as well. His parents in Žilina would hardly have liked to hear that his foster father in Norway was now a prominent Nazi. Perhaps Edgar in that case would have been recalled, as were two of the other Jewish children in Bergen at this time.

Rea Brichta of course, had heard from him now that Norway was in the war. That's why she asked Agnes Normann about getting a letter at least every second or third week.

> I hope you do not consider my desire to be immodest, because you surely understand that I am now more anxious than ever when I hear nothing for long periods.

Now Edgar also took to writing a letter to Žilina. Early in the New Year 1941, date unknown, came the answer. Mother Rea thanked him so much for his letter. She also thanked God that her son still was safe and well. She did worry that Edgar's German skills now began to fail, and exhorted him to keep up with the language: "Can you not get German books to read up there?" She did however praise him for having remembered to congratulate Vera on her birthday, and his mother warned him now that his father's birthday is imminent. Otherwise, the letter gave the impression that the three were in good spirits. One hint revealed that all was not well: "We no longer have your hens. There was no food for them now."

The stamps with cancelation marks of swastikas on the envelope showed that the letter was opened and checked by *Sonderkommando der Wehrmacht.* It may also explain why the contents of the last letters were more trivial than in the past.

Agnes thus was the one who mostly took care of Edgar. She arranged things with the school, had contact with the Nansen Council and also with Rea Brichta. Arne was rarely involved in such things, although he certainly helped her with the German language, and sent greetings in the letters to Slovakia. Edgar did not think a lot about his parents initially during his time in Norway. There were so many new impressions that he had absorbed and processed. But he remembers that he often thought of his little sister. Among other things, he cut out strips of comics Stomperud and Knoll and Tott (Beetle Bailey and The Katzenjammer Kids) and pasted them into notebooks. The text he translated to show to Vera when they met again.

Edgar remembers Agnes as a lovable woman. They shared an interest in plants, flowers and birds, and listened to music together. Agnes made a suit for him out of the material from Arne's old military uniform - green and totally indestructible. He was so proud of the suit that he wore it almost every day. His friends can barely remember him without it.

At one point during that time Agnes asked Edgar also what was his favorite food at his home in Bratislava. The answer was 'a kind of plum dumpling' served with butter and ground nuts. Agnes found the recipe in a magazine, where it correctly was called Austrian, and Edgar was impressed when he got home to find dumplings served in a Nygårdsvik kitchen.

His relationship with his foster father was never poor. But after Arne Normann took over as mayor, his mood was unstable. He experienced growing opposition from his community to an extent he could not have anticipated. Edgar perceived him later as a naive idealist, one who thought he was doing the right thing, but did not understand what he had embarked on. Many did what they could to make life miserable for collaborators. If his mood was good, Arne responded laconically on real, or imaginary, provocations. If his mood was worse, he was bitter. Several times he reported people who irritated him to the police and petitioned to have them punished. He was made to pay for this at his trial for treason.

In his mayoral assignment Arne Normann received support from an experienced, former Labor party politician, who now had joined the NS. Still Arne struggled a lot, showing uncertain leadership and inability to accomplish tasks. The governor - the occupying power's local manager of municipalities - complained several times on the expiration of deadlines. Some of this was due to the fact that Arne was opposed by close associates. The office manager, Laksevåg municipality's top bureaucrat, carried on a verbal guerrilla war against his unwelcome boss, something several sarcastic letters in the municipal archives testify. Arne got him fired in 1941.Then he himself assumed the office manager's job and thus became both the political and the administrative leader of the community.

It was not the only time he fired people - or refused to hire them - because of their negative attitude toward the "new arrangement", which he used to call the occupation. The National Union's (NS) centralized leadership team did not demand that public employees be members of the party, but still expected "active participation in the spirit of the NS", as it was outlined in a1940 article in the *Free People* (Norway's Nazi newspaper). Those who did not exhibit the proper enthusiasm of the day, were considered to be disloyal to the service. Thus Arne Normann did as he was told, even if NS could hardly claim any employer responsibility for all public employees. Arne followed up with a circular, after the message arrived from Oslo that all public employees should subscribe to *Free People.* Also, that the only permissible polite ending of any letter was to be 'Heil og Sael' ('Hail and Health', equivalent to 'Heil Hitler' in Germany). The ones not displaying proper enthusiasm for these guidelines were to be considered unreliable workers. In view of this what Arne Normann did was in keeping with the directives he received, even though the Nazis could hardly claim being responsible for all public employees.

Arne Normann also tried - without much success - to command his agency heads to go and listen to NS-leaders on lecture tours. Arne did however also display independent ideological initiative. Mayoral correspondence shows that he was often observant of potential propaganda benefits of some decisions and events, and the danger of the opposite in other cases.

The requisition of rubber boots for German soldiers on the Eastern Front in 1942 can stand as an example of how the job of mayor at times was both a comical triviality, and on how heavy and serious the matter nonetheless could be. The starting point was in itself hard enough for Arne Normann. The Germans were on the defensive in the war, and his own position was correspondingly exposed. The soldiers needed more blankets, sleeping bags, backpacks and rubber boots than they could get from home. Therefore such things were requisitioned from people in the occupied countries to be sent to the front.

The local historical commemorative book *That was it II* tells of an episode that unfolded after it was announced that all rubber boots size 41 or over must be turned in. Bjørn Gravdal of Laksevåg had a couple of expensive, heavy rubber boots in size 47 that he simply would not give up. He therefore failed to report the boots. But soon a serious letter came from the Laksevåg municipality, signed by Mayor Arne Normann arrived. After describing the regulation and its purpose, the mayor writes, "In reference to the information that we have here, you are in the possession of rubber boots which you have not declared". Gravdal was further told that this could lead to "punishment according to German law", but he would be given an opportunity "to arrange immediately to meet in my office and give an explanation, and to bring your rubber boots."

Bjørn Gravdal did not give up the fight. He met with the mayor the day after, with the boots, but pointed out how big they were. Size 47 could not possibly be of use at the front? According to Gravdal, Arne Normann examined and measured the boots before he went out to an adjoining office. After a while he came back with the message that he had conferred with the German authorities, and they had concluded that the boots, because of their size, had to be considered irrelevant. So Gravdal got to keep his boots and left satisfied.

Arne Normann had other things to think about. Certainly one could push people to submit equipment for soldiers on the front, but they were promised a financial settlement in return. By and by, as the Germans' problems piled up, it became increasingly difficult to get them to fork out compensations. In letter after letter the mayor urged *Reichskommissar Dienststelle Bergen* to pay up:

> It is most unfortunate that these people do not get a quick and easy settlement of the requisitioned items. These difficulties (...) naturally create dissatisfaction and confusion. One thinks that, particularly at this time, it is of very great importance to avoid these kinds of unnecessary difficulties.

No doubt who was scolded in regard to this matter.

Not everything Arne Normann did as mayor contributed to a negative reputation. He attentively authorized "'potato holidays", so employees could scrounge for extra food. He also had a continuing struggle to obtain for Laksevåg families a place to live as replacements for properties requisitioned by the "protective power". He was also wary of the NS members that took the party book in hand in order to gain special advantages in the municipality. An NS man in the county service was caught for embezzlement, fired and reported to the police. Arne often felt very frustrated and alone. A letter, filed in the county archives, to governor Astrup testifies:

> ...it's not enough that I have difficulty in all respects with the sabotage of current officials and the workers' side, but I also have difficulties with those who represent the National Unity.

Indignation is evident in much of the correspondence, and occasionally also attacks against those the Nazis felt were the cause of all problems in the world: the Jews. The climax, if this word can be used, came when Arne Normann in April 1943 wrote a letter to the Norwegian Broadcasting Corporation's (Norsk Rikskringkastings, abbr. NRK) program branch in Bergen. NRK was governed by NS during the war and Laksevåg's mayor had a treat for the editors. He suggested that they interview a particular NS Member of Laksevåg who "had spent most of his time in America primarily as a mate aboard yachts belonging to wealthy Americans."

> The following facts should be mentioned. NN (the author's *wish to keep the anonymity)* has served these Jewish dollar kings who are known throughout the world: The Copper King Guggenheimer, B.M. Baruch who during the First World War was President Wilson's right hand, the movie mogul Jed. Harris, film actor Lewis Stone and others. (...)
>
> It's pretty amazing the things NN can tell of these dollarkings' private life and today I guess the issue would certainly be of interest for broadcasting either in transmissions for sailors or in broadcasts here at home, and I would recommend that the broadcasters get in touch with the person concerned.

In the neighborhood of his home in Nygårdsvik, Arne Normann was still perceived as a fairly moderate NS-man, who was not particularly aggressive, with a wife who was well liked and certainly not an NS member. Arne was not popular in the district, and he had not been before the war. He was perceived as a rather sullen and distant man. Also the fact that he was an engineer created a certain distance. But he was good to have sometimes. His neighbor Liv Bergsfjord tells that Normann was the only one in the neighborhood who had a telephone, and it could be borrowed by neighbors when needed. One evening while there was a curfew, a woman in the neighborhood had an urgent need to get to another house at some distance. Arne took it on to follow her. As mayor he was permitted to move about during curfew hours.

Edgar did notice that Arne's mood turned increasingly irritable throughout the war. Only once he remembers his foster father really angry. It was when the two went up to a small patch of land at Nygård to reap what they had planted of cabbage and kohlrabi. Once they arrived, it turned out that someone had let cattle go into the field and eat up everything. Arne was convinced that the culprit was the farmer from whom Arne had leased the land. Arne who had no proof of this came with a powerful tirade about how people thought they could behave. Another time Arne brought Edgar along on a trip to Stokmarknes to visit Arne's parents and siblings. The *Hurtigruta*,(the coastal passenger ship) sailed north along the coast. Each time the boat docked, passengers had some time to go ashore. Arne knew the timetable by heart, and thought he had full control. But when they got back to the pier after looking at Måløy, (or maybe it was Ålesund), the ship had left minutes early and was now some distance from the shore. Arne waved and shouted. Eventually he was able to hail a leisure motorboat to catch up with the *Hurtigruta* ship that had cut the engine for him. This, too, Arne saw as a harassment of himself. He believed that the only reason the *Hurtigruta* slowed down as the small motorboat raced to catch up was that Arne's father was a member of the board of directors of the shipping company, Vesterålske Dampskips Selskap, owner of the ship. This Arne also saw as a snub for being a NS mayor.

Chapter 6

At the outbreak of WWII there lived about 2100 Jews in Norway. They knew what was happening on the continent, but had felt relatively safe in neutral Norway.

What now when the German military power thundered in even here? The fear must have been great. Initially not much happened. Apart from confiscating all radios from Jews in May 1940, of course this was bad enough, but the occupying force undertook no general restrictions for the first 18 months. The country's two Jewish congregations, in Trondheim and Oslo, mostly continued their activities. Most Jewish businessmen could also continue their activities undisturbed. Some Jews with ties to Germany and Poland, however were still subjected to unpleasant attention from the police. In Bergen, five Jewish men were repeatedly brought in and interrogated by the anti-Semite Gerhard Flesch, head of the German Security Police in the city. He was among other things concerned about any Jews wanted by German authorities. Three of the Jewish men were also detained in the late autumn of 1940 together with resistance fighters and other prisoners in Ulven camp by Os, where Flesch came visiting to bully them. In October 1941, Gerhard Flesch was transferred to a similar position in the German security police in Trondheim, where he initiated a systematic confiscation of Jewish businesses.

On the whole it was the quiet before the storm. Not even in everyday life were there signs of rising anti-Semitism. Jews were reviled in Nazi newspapers, but there were few people who read them. One particular episode however stirred up a lot of talk in Bergen. In January 1941, the German-born Jew Ernst Glaser was invited by the Music society, Harmonien, for a performance as soloist in the Concert Palace, in a program of music by Haydn, Sinding, Graener and Ole Bull. Glaser was a violinist and Concertmaster of the Philharmonic Society Orchestra in Oslo. He had been a guest performer in Bergen several times before. Newspaper announcements informed that Glaser would perform on the instrument of Ole Bull. This particularly turned out to create reactions.

The following day the conservative newspaper *Bergens Aftenblad* (Bergen's Evening paper) described what had happened at the filled to capacity Konsertpaleet (Concert palace) on the evening of January 16:

> At the midpoint of the performance of Harmonien's concert yesterday the management of Harmonien received information from a group of N.S. youth stating that demonstrations would be activated if the evening's soloist were to perform. The given reason was that he is Jewish, and one considered it a sacrilege of a national treasure if he played with the violin of Ole Bull.

Under these circumstances the management of Harmonien decided it prudent to terminate the concert. It was assigned to the conductor to announce this to the audience. The cancelation created considerable indignation and was received with expressions of displeasure. At the confusion that rose in the hall there were, from the gallery, thrown pamphlets wherein the origins and circumstances of the soloist were outlined.

The Bergen Aftenblad added that the incident was "exceedingly regrettable", it was assumed that the National Unity (NS) management had nothing to do with the action, and that the perpetrators were "young people who could not estimate the magnitude of their actions".

The newspaper was courageous, as the Bergen press had been given instructions not to mention the incident. Only one of the other newspapers mentioned it, and then in an indirect way and careful choice of words. This is told by the historian Per Kristian Sebak in his book about the Jews in Bergen. Additionally he also wrote that the report to the police by the Harmonien and complaint to the ministry of Culture and public education did not lead to anything even though the perpetrators' identities were known. The National Unity (NS) leadership requested the Ministry to take action against the Harmonien for inviting a Jewish artist, but this also was not acted upon. Sebak also tells that some members of the NS in Bergen regretted the action against Glaser.

The author Olav Mosby reported of the drama in the Philharmonic in a book already in 1945. According to him, the incident was

> ...the standing topic of conversation in town for a considerable length of time afterwards. It had made a strong impression on people, and one could discern enormous exasperation everywhere.

October 2, 1941 came the first attempt at a general action against the Jews. The Justice Minister Sverre Riisnæs requested the nation's governors to prepare and submit an inventory of all real estate property owned by persons of Jewish descent. The county Governor of Hordaland and Bergen sent a circular on to the two counties' local and regional authorities. All responded saying that they were unaware of any properties in Jewish possession, writes Sebak.

At this time the carnage had already been implemented a considerably long time further south in Europe. Shortly after the start of the new year on January 20, 1942, 13 leading German officials also met in Wannsee outside of Berlin "to prepare for the final solution of the Jewish problem". The meeting, which lasted for only one day, has remained as the seal for the fate of the European Jews. Hereafter, one would no longer hurry to pursue the Jews to kill them. They should be gathered and sent to camps specially designed for that purpose. The meeting was chaired by SS-General Reinhard Heydrich, head of the Reichssicherheitshauptamt (RSHA) {National security central office} which included the Gestapo, and also the national protectorate of Bohemia and Moravia. Also present were Adolf Eichmann, head of the German Secret Police for Jewish affairs, as well as Dr. Martin Luther, Deputy State Secretary of the Foreign Ministry in Berlin. According to the protocol, the latter took the matter up in Denmark and Norway exclusively. Luther advised against taking care of the Jewish problem as thoroughly in these countries, because then difficulties could arise. He recommended temporarily not to go "to such extensive operations" here, adding "considering the low number of Jews a postponement would not cause any limitations."

In Slovakia, on the other hand, measures were seriously implemented against the almost 90,000 Jews. Already in the fall of 1941, the regime of Jozef Tiso moved towards that goal. All Jews had to wear a visible star of David when they were outdoors. Increasingly, property of Jews was being confiscated. Admittedly the Slovaks were still somewhat lenient in the German's eyes, in that certain groups of Jews were excluded, such as the Jews who still worked in public services. Moreover, they just now introduced the measures that had long been in force in Germany: Jews were forbidden to drive cars, they could ride the train only in third class, could not work in certain professions, and so on. On the other hand, the Slovaks struck with a measure not even the Germans had thought of: All letters sent by Jews were stamped with a star of David, and the police could both control and destroy them. Sending postcards was also forbidden.

Max and Rea Brichta in Žilina naturally experienced this themselves. Letters north contained steadily fewer substantive data and (at least it can be comprehended in retrospect) increasingly assumed optimism. In an undated letter, but probably sent in December 1941, Rea Brichta thanks so much for the letter they received recently from Agnes, and wished the Normann couple, all their loved ones, and Edgar a merry Christmas and a happy new year.

> God willing, next year we get the long-awaited peace so that we can get together joyfully and spend a some days together. My husband has long planned to write to thank you for your kindness, but he is unfortunately just as lazy as the letter writer as Edgar, it remains always with the good resolutions.

An additional message from Edgar's mother contained some reprimands. She would namely "also like to have a letter from you soon". However, Vera age six wrote with newly learned cursive:

> Dear Aunt Normann and dear Edgar! I wish you nice holidays and send many kisses. Vera

On the paper she drew a house with a picket fence, a Christmas tree, another tree and a sun. It was the only drawing Edgar got from his little sister.

A new letter to Edgar dated January 13, 1942 also just had simple everyday information, without characterization. The only exception was that Rea mentioned that the postcards she and Edgar's grandmother were going to send as a New Year's greeting were not accepted by the post office. They thanked Edgar for finally having sent a letter again after a long silence. Again they noted his failing German, and told him to shape up. But they promised to get letters translated from Norwegian should it become necessary. Little sister Vera wrote a greeting, obviously excited about her new school life:

> Dear Edgar. I've already got my grades and they are awesome. What kind of grades did you get? Write to me sometime. Greetings and kisses from Vera. Many greetings also to my dear aunt and uncle Normann.

March 16, 1942, a new envelope came to Nygårdsvik. Now his parents had written each a separate letter. Recently Edgar had obviously told that he was good at skiing, for Max Brichta wondered if his son had also attempted to ski jump. Max thanked Edgar for Vera for the pictures he sent from Norway. Maybe Edgar also complained a little about something in Nygårdsvik; he got another dose of admonitions to behave:

> Dear Edgar, if you are fond of Vera, your mother and father, never show defiance. You're a decent guy and you will understand that you will be happier if you are docile. Do not worry about it; just do as engineer and Mrs. Normann say. I just have to say that both Mrs. and engineer Normann are very, very good people who helped you and us very much.

Whereas his father, surely because of the strict censorship, stayed clear of anything that could characterize the living situation of the family in Žilina, mother Rea gave what was perhaps a disguised glimpse into the realities. As usual, Edgar was asked to write soon, but the reason was new: "... because we do not know how long we get to remain here".

Since everything else in the letters sounded so ordinary, these words are not enough to unsettle a robust boy of 12. But the two letters turned out to be the last ones to find their way from Žilina to Nygårdsvik. The first transport of Jews from Slovakia to Auschwitz and other extermination camps was March 26, 1942, ten days after the postmark date.

Although the German Nazi chiefs at the Wannsee meeting did not think it was urgent to take the Jews in Norway, the occupying power worked in Oslo to get an overview of how many they were and where they lived. It was slow going, and January 20, 1942 – incidentally the same day as the Wannsee meeting was arranged - Police sent out an announcement that all Jews had to report to the police, so a 'J' could be stamped in their identification papers. The deadline was set for March 1, and most of the country's Jews dared not but follow the order. But there were some exceptions. Neither Edgar nor any of the other children who had come to the Bergen area from Prague and

Bratislava in October 1939 ended up on the list. The reason must be that the foster parents were warned not to do it, by Aslaug Blytt and others on the Nansenhelp local committee.

Already in 1940 the Nansen Hjelp examined the possibility of having the children sent to neutral Sweden. Conditions in Norway became increasingly difficult, and besides, this group of Jewish refugee children had been thoroughly exposed in the media. Everyone had to know about them. Additionally the Nansen Council local leader, Aslaug Blytt, and her family were so involved in resistance work on a broad front, that she was a risk factor herself. Thus, there was reason to believe that the German security police had both her and the children in their sight. But it was not possible to obtain exit permits. Now, in January 1942, it was therefore decided to advise the foster parents not to raise the issue of their children's J-stamp, and all followed the advice. Also Agnes Normann must have been contacted about the case, and most likely she was asked not to raise the issue with the mayor of Laksevåg. Knowing how the relationship was between them, it's hard to believe that Agnes did not consult Arne. But it's possible. The requirement for registration received little attention, so it may have gone unnoticed by Arne. The ladies of the Nansenhjelp may have been insistent with Agnes.

Between the announcement and its deadline, Vidkun Quisling became head of the government in Norway - with his new title of Minister President. The new government from February 1, 1942 would still share power with Reichskommissar Terboven and his people. Neither the registration nor the political reorganization had any immediate consequences for the Jews. Children continued to go to school, people kept working on the job, most businesses could continue operating. But now the Nazi authorities had an overview of who the Jews were and where they lived. In Oslo people wondered what the list of Jews would be used for.

The revelation came in the autumn. The first wave of mass arrests was carried out October 26, 1942. All adult men with J-stamp identification papers were to be arrested at six o'clock that morning. Officials from the Norwegian state police and from local police stations followed the order. The same day Minister President Vidkun Quisling also sanctioned the "Law on confiscation of property belonging to Jews", and this should be implemented immediately. The law came - it was announced in the media the following day – "as a natural result of the battle currently in progress between the Axis powers on the one side and the Jewish world on the other".

In Bergen, all the 13 Jewish men on the list were found in their homes on the morning of October 26, and thrown in jail by the Bergen Police on All Saints' Street 3. Later, most were sent to Berg detention camp outside Tønsberg. On November 7 Quisling decided to release all over age 65. Thus, three men from Bergen got to return home again.

Liberty for these three lasted for two and a half weeks. On November 25th, an order was issued for all remaining Jews, regardless of age and gender, to be apprehended. Now all the Jews in Norway were included in the Nazi's Endlösung (final solution). The arrest order was issued by the chief of the German security police in Norway. He had made arrangements for a special ship, the Donau, to carry the Jews to Germany. And so on to the concentration camps, where the gas chambers were awaiting. All Jewish children deported from Norway in the autumn of 1942 and winter of 1943 ended up in Auschwitz and were, like most of the adults, immediately gassed to death.

How could people look at this calmly? In some cases, also in Bergen, Jewish schoolchildren literally were pulled out of classrooms. What the Jews risked, ought by now to have been generally known. Had the stress of the war become so strong that people did not react anymore? Leo Eitinger, one of those who survived the German extermination camps, came later with a conciliatory statement:

> It was not only understandable, there was something humane about this naivete which posterity cannot understand. For fortunately it was not in the Norwegians'

> character to imagine that someone would pull a ten-year old girl, a Nygård school student, out from her home on Møhlenprisbakken, drag her through half of Europe and kill her in one of the industrial gas chambers.

The nine children, who at the time were still under the supervision of Nansenhjelpen in Bergen, were not on the arrest list. The absence of a J-stamp on their identification papers sheltered them from the ruthless intervention. But this neither they nor their guardians could have known then, and other events at this time created great anxiety. This is written in Aslaug Blytt's and Hildur Andersen's report after the war:

> In November 1942, shortly after the Germans had launched their persecution of Jews in Norway, Nansenhjelpen's children's committee in Bergen got a message from Nansenhjelpen, Oslo, about Nansenhjelpen's records having been seized by Nazi authorities, and that one had to prepare for letting the children go under cover and send them to Sweden.

So this was after the first round of arrests, where all Jewish men were taken. It triggered the alarm at Nansenhjelpen in Bergen - maybe the occupation authorities would soon come to get women and children also? The fear that the raid in Oslo had given the Gestapo an address list of the children in the Bergen area, was exaggerated. Nansenhjelpen people in Oslo were not so amateurish. Odd Nansen writes in *Along the Road* that the Gestapo combed through their offices and archives as early as April or May 1940, without finding any compromising material.

> The only thing that might have interested them, the addresses of the refugees' living locations, we had removed in time. We explained to the Gestapos that after the occupation, the children had all left their abodes a while ago and were scattered to the winds beyond our control.

The Gestapo raid in November 1942 - while Nansen himself sat arrested in Grini [a prison camp in Bærum, Norway] - ceased Nansenhjelpen's key activities. But the Gestapos did not find anything they could use either. The alarm signal over the mountains, probably sent by Sigrid Helliesen Lund, dealt with something of a somewhat different nature: The action in Oslo suggested that the pursuit of refugees was stepped up, and that it was therefore prudent to get as many as possible over the border to Sweden.

In any event Aslaug Blytt, Bergljot Horne and the others started to plan for the evacuation of the children to the neutral neighbor nation in the east. Foster parents were approached quietly, and escape routes were outlined. The Bergen branch provided transport to Oslo, where Sigrid Helliesen Lund's people took over the most difficult job, to get them illegally across the national border. From mid-December 1942 to mid January 1943 Nansenhjelpen, Bergen, sent eight kids off. A few weeks later came confirmation from Sweden that they had arrived safely and that everything was in order.

Only Edgar was not evacuated. Nansenhjelpen dared not take the chance. In a report by Hildur Andersen and Aslaug Blytt, it was explained this way:

> The 9th child, Edgar Brichta, remained as stated in Norway. His foster father had become a Nazi, and therefore Edgar's travel had to be postponed until the other children arrived safely. One feared that otherwise they could risk a reporting by the foster father, that would expose both the children and their caregivers to unnecessary danger.

Nansenhjelpen was going to get Edgar out immediately after the risky evacuation of the other eight was completed. But then Aslaug Blytt was arrested by the German security police. She and the others in the Nansen Council feared at first that the work regarding the Jewish children was the reason, but it turned out quickly that Blytt was arrested because of other resistance work. She was let out not long after.

Only the birds would know what was said between Agnes and Arne Normann during this period in Nygårdsvik while Edgar was not within earshot. Agnes must have been contacted by Nansenhjelpen when the order for registration of the Jews came, so that Edgar was not taken to the police to get the "J" stamped on his papers. Probably Agnes was also later in contact with Aslaug Blytt or Bergljot Horne.

We do not know if Agnes and Arne discussed the case when the registration was on the daily agenda. Possibly Arne was so involved with the job of mayor that he was unaware of the announcement. But when the deportation of Jews was implemented, which Arne certainly did not miss, he and Agnes did talk. Did she then insist on saving Edgar, by "coercing" her husband, perhaps under pressure from the ladies of the Nansenhjelpen? It's hard to know. Viewed by others, Agnes did not appear as forceful in relation to Arne. On the other hand the norm at that time was that men were in charge even in a marriage, and in any case it had to appear that way.

Agnes and Boris.

She may have had a stronger position in relation to her spouse in situations when neither their children nor others were present.

Arne Normann's exposed position as NS-mayor placed him under severe pressure. He was hated and opposed by many in the local community, which also bothered him. This may have made him particularly attentive to Agnes' wishes. He could not very well risk getting her against him also. On the other hand, Arne obviously risked a strong reaction from the power structure he was a part of. If the NS-management or the Reichskommissar discovered that he hid a Jew in his home, he would have been severely punished, especially now that the deportations were in progress.

The adopted daughter Anne remembers that her mother told her something about this in the 1960s. Agnes said that she and Arne had discussed sending Edgar to Sweden, which must have been in connection with Nansenhjelpen's evacuation operation in the autumn of 1942. "But we decided to keep him. Another Jew was staying in hiding in the neighborhood, so we felt that it was safe enough", Anne remembers Agnes saying

Who this other Jew may have been in or near Nygårdsvik is unknown, but if Agnes was candid here with her daughter, it suggests that Arne consciously and actively helped to keep Edgar from being deported following a discussion in which their foster son's care and their own safety were the main topics.

It is possible to imagine Arne Normann as a hero, that is, he actively contributed so that the nine Czechs and Slovaks were "forgotten" when the occupation authorities in the Bergen area executed orders from Oslo. The history of World War II is filled with accounts of large and small heroic deeds carried out by people within the power structures. But in Arne's case this is quite unlikely. He had hardly a strong enough position in the local NS environment to do that. Nor does anything suggest that he was ever bothered by scruples in relation to his undertaking. His hatred of Jews is beyond doubt.

Less unlikely is that another member of the local NS community helped Arne keep silent about Edgar and the others. We do not know whether Arne discussed the topic with someone he trusted in the party, but it would not be surprising. Per Kristian Sebak writes there were some other Jews in Bergen whose names did not get placed on the list in 1942, thus avoiding the deportation. In the Bergen area - it turned out later –there was never an intense persecution of Jews who had escaped the J-stamp on their papers. There were surely several reasons for this. But one of them could be that in Bergen people have always been willing to oppose any demands originating in Oslo. This also applied to several of the local NS heads during the war. Sebak writes that among others, "the NS press chief, the NS propaganda leader of the party and several of the party (NS) police officers partially or completely sabotaged orders from Oslo." The German authorities in Oslo observed the NS Party in Bergen with "increasing skepticism", according to a letter cited by the historian. Whether this peculiarity [of not following NS orders] helped to save Edgar is impossible to know. But there is evidence that Jews elsewhere in the country were identified and sent to their death in Germany as late as the autumn of 1943.

Arne Normann must have been strongly perplexed about how to proceed. He had attached himself emotionally to Edgar and would not hurt the boy, but he was certainly also aware that by hiding him he made himself guilty of gross misconduct. Arne was probably a Norwegian version of those SS chief Heinrich Himmler spoke of scornfully in his famous speech at an internal meeting of SS officers in Poznan [a city in west-central Poland] in 1941:

> This is among the things we say so readily: "The Jewish people will be exterminated", says every Party comrade. "Quite clearly, it is written in our program. Jews have got to disappear. Exterminated. We will do it. Ha - a trifle!"
>
> But then come all the 80 million good Germans, and each one has his decent Jew. They say: All the others are swine, but here we have an excellent Jew.

Edgar knew nothing about all this drama, and was more keen to make new friends. On the way from central Laksevåg to Nygårdsvik, German soldiers had forbidden people to walk on the right side of a section of the way. They should in fact not be able to look down on Nygårdsmyren where the Germans kept Russian prisoners of war. Those who defied the ban could be fired at. Bullet holes in the window of the dairy buildings on the other side of the road gave clear proof of this. The condition for those, up to 1500 prisoners, concerned people throughout Laksevåg. The emaciated, ragged Russians were especially visible as they were escorted every morning in columns towards the sheet metal rolling mill and other work assignments, and then back again in the evening. When the chance arose, people gave them some food, and as thanks some of the prisoners carved wooden figures and decorated cans in appreciation. Several Russians prisoners were shot during the time of war, some in attempts to escape, and others during an uprising when they hoisted a red flag in the camp.

Contact with prisoners was prohibited and dangerous. Children still had some freedom of movement. Once Edgar and one of his friends came along with a wheelbarrow with food waste for a 'villa pig'. As they came past a column of Russians being led from the work site to the Nygårdsmyren camp, some of the Russians reached down in the wheelbarrow and put food waste into their jacket pockets, others ate some on the fly. Near the sheet metal rolling mill, the kids could sometimes come close to the prisoners of war. Some German guards were more lenient than others, and Edgar was able to approach close. Sometimes he brought food for the prisoners if Agnes - despite

German machine gun post on Dokkeskjærskaien in Bergen, April 1940. (Photo: War archives / SCANPIX.)

shortages and rationing - had something to spare. From the Russians, he learned a few words and simple sentences with which, as his friends recalled, he impressed them. He also remembers that he got wooden figurines. One was a plywood figure of a gymnast that could swing between parallel sticks of wood.

Edgar repeated his success from Nordfjordeid, by becoming familiar with some of the occupiers. One of them, the Austrian Wehrmacht man Gabauer, he met several times. The story is told in the first chapter of this book. Exactly when this happened is not known. Edgar thinks it was relatively late during his stay in Laksevåg. His bold independence also suggests that it probably occurred in late 1942. If so, Arne Normann's reaction is also easy to understand, for this was the phase when the Jews were taken, and the risk of hiding them was probably higher than ever before.

Again we wonder how in the world could a Jewish boy scuttle around in this way, without ever having to be told to keep his Jewish identity to himself. Edgar is certain that neither the foster parents, nor care provider Bergljot Horne ever admonished him about this. His own theory is that the adults considered him so unruly, that they feared it could be counterproductive.

Edgar was conscious that he was Jewish, but it was not something he thought about daily. There were few Jews in Bergen, and fewer as time went by. He only met a few, not the children he had fled the country with. Moreover, the newspapers were censored now. He did not hear about the deportations and evacuation of the other Jewish children to Sweden until later. He lived at risk every day, but knew nothing of it.

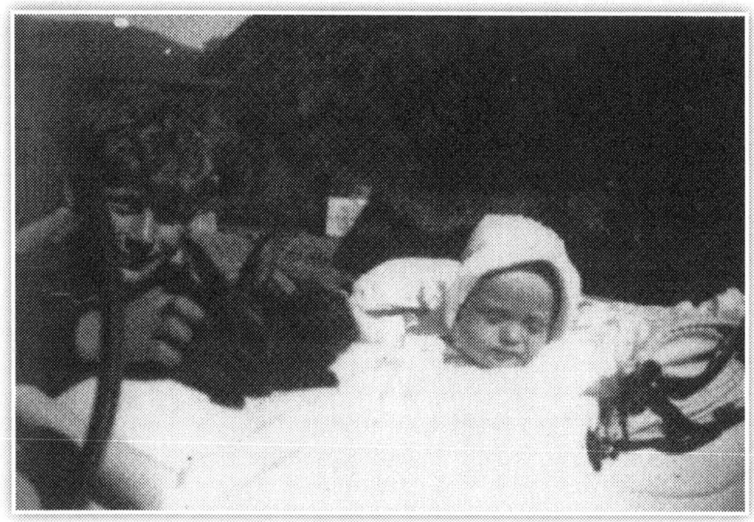

Edgar and Anne in 1942 with rabbit mother, Hanni.

In the autumn of 1942, World War II was at its hottest. The Germans had had problems in the year old war against the Soviet Union. With the attack on Pearl Harbor in Hawaii, Japan brought the United States into the war in full swing. The British raided Cologne with a thousand aircraft. Large parts of the world were now involved. Although there was much evidence that the Germans were on the defensive, on August 19, 1942 Adolf Hitler nevertheless gave his 6th Army the order to attack Stalingrad. Three days later, Arne Normann sought out the German military authorities to volunteer for military service. Whether he would offer his life to Adolf Hitler in the hour of destiny or whether he was mostly tired of the annoyance of the mayor's office is uncertain.

On a couple of occasions in 1941 and 1942, he offered to enter active service in the Norwegian legion on the eastern front. Neither of these offers was accepted, possibly because the NS party leadership and the Reichskommissar's people in Bergen thought he was more useful kept in Laksevåg.

Later, in the fall, Agnes and Arne decided to adopt a girl. Edgar went with Agnes to the orphanage in Milde to pick up the girl She was named Anne Emilie Normann. Not long after Nansensenhjelpen was asked to find new foster parents for Edgar. Why? There were probably several reasons why as there was tension in the house in Nygårdsvik. After the tough year of 1942, Arne Normann may have wanted to get rid of the risk of having Edgar. Edgar's foster sister Anne told him many years later that Agnes Normann had once given her an idea of what the main reason had been. Agnes had asked Edgar how he felt about Anne coming to live with them. "I think you should let her stay at the orphanage", Edgar said darkly, and he thinks that account is accurate.

Edgar might have been jealous of no longer having the full attention and showed signs of dissatisfaction. Agnes asked him if he would like to stay somewhere else, and Edgar said yes. Aslaug Blytt and the others in the Nansen Council must have cheered with relief - now they could move Edgar without risk of provoking Arne Normann.

After being the adults' pawn for 12 years, Edgar now started - sometime between the end of 1942 and the beginning of 1943- to take care of himself.

Chapter 7

Bergljot Horne picked up Edgar from Nygårdsvik, on May 20, 1943. They walked together down to the ferry dock to get across to Bergen. Boris went down to the pier, and must have realized that his playmate was about to leave. The dog wanted strenuously to board, and had to be held back by force. Edgar followed Boris with his eyes on the way out of Damsgårdssundet, and this was the last time he saw the dog. Boris did not in fact return to the house in Nygårdsvik either. During a later visit with Agnes and Arne, Edgar was told about the disappearance and search for Boris. Some had seen the dog being dragged away by two German marines. Arne Normann had then gone to the German garrison and demanded to get his dog back, but there he was brusquely rejected. The incident was hard on all three, particularly Arne, who was upset that the Germans could treat him - a loyal mayor - in this way.

Dr. Horne first brought Edgar south to Store Milde in Fana, which like Laksevåg was not part of Bergen yet. Bergljot Horne had her residence and medical practice in Store Markevei 4b in Bergen seized by the German Gestapo. The Germans used the house to accommodate personnel. Now Bergljot stayed in a fairly plain cabin in Fana, where she also accommodated Edgar while she and her colleagues in the Nansenhjelpen kept looking for new foster parents.

Bergljot Horne was partly in the shadow of the great resistance woman in the Bergen area, Aslaug Blytt, but she was also active in the fight against the German occupation, not only through Nansenhjelpen. Bergljot was a great supporter of King Haakon VII. She often told about the time she had been in a grocery store in Oslo, and heard a tall Danish-speaking man ask for a kilogram of bananas. It was the King himself. Bergljot also knew the poet Herman Wildenvey from her home village of Eiker. Her descendants still have the first volume of *Total Poems* from 1927, with a dedication: "Dr. Bergljot Horne Maisey. The most beautiful flower from our shared home village. Herm. Wildenvey".

Bergljot was married to an older British naval officer, Harry Maisey, who traveled home to the safety of the UK when the war broke out. They had son, George, together. He was just a little younger than Edgar, and the two quickly became good friends. This helped Edgar to have a good time at the cottage in Milde. George and he had a permanent job to fetch water from the well. Edgar found also an outlet for his botanical interest by planting flowers along the trail that went from the cabin down to the main road. Bergljot had a great liking for crime novels. When she visited bookstores and staff asked what she was looking for, she used to answer "a cozy crime novel". In the evenings he read some of Bergljot's many mystery novels. Once he experienced that some pages were glued together in places where the stories were the most exciting. George had done it in revenge for whatever Edgar had said or done that annoyed George.

Although the cottage was modest, the busy physician had the help of a maid keeping the house clean and tidy. George and Edgar were comfortable. One day Edgar saw Bergljot Horne outside burning some of her books. The explanation proved to be fairly unique. The young maid had developed a rash and sores, and lost much of her hair. It turned out that the girl had been with a sailor on her voyage from Northern Norway and apparently become infected with syphilis by him. This was before antibiotics were available, so the girl had to be sent to the hospital. And

Edgar and George quickly became good friends. Here in the courtyard of Bergljot's residence in Store Markevei 4b in 1946. The building had been in German possession during the war.

thus here stood Dr. Bergljot Horne burning books which she thought the maid had handled, even though the doctor said it would be most unlikely that any book could have been made contagious. Syphilis is transmitted only through body fluids. Edgar remembers the maid as enjoyable and lively, if somewhat forward, and he felt sorry for her. She never returned to the housekeeping job at Doctor Horne's.

A slightly older maid Bergljot employed later also was fired when it was revealed that she had fraternized with German soldiers.

Edgar was now 13, and thus mature enough to comprehend the information he received in a different way than before. Still the war was - in his words - first and foremost an adventure, but gradually increasing in gravity. During the first half of 1943 the war leaned in favor of the Allies, although no one could be certain about this. In January, the leaders of Germany's opponents met at a summit in Casablanca. From there, the U.S. President Franklin D. Roosevelt demanded The Third Reich's unconditional surrender. The bloody battle of Stalingrad ended with the Germans giving up resistance in

February. In April and May, uprisings raged in the Warsaw ghetto, and the Germans eventually leveled the area with the earth and killed almost all the Jews there. In May additionally, Germany and its allies also were defeated in North Africa. All this came out

Bergljot Horne and husband Harry Maisey. Edgar lived a period in 1943, at Bergljot's place in Milde. Harry Maisey was in England. The photograph is from Harry's 80th birthday in 1968. Bergljot was a doctor and active in the Nansenhjelpen and Harry was a British naval officer(retired).

poorly in the censored Norwegian media, but Bergljot Horne received information through illegal channels from active resistance fighters.

Bergljot did not tell Edgar about the resistance work she partook in while the war was ongoing. Until many years later, she only gave small glimpses into the subject, for example, when she in a letter - and almost in passing - said that she then had received instructions from the Home Front via the postman. But any extra information about the war Edgar accrued from other sources. Bergljot told him, moreover, that the other children who came with him from Czechoslovakia were sent to neutral Sweden in 1942. Edgar did not even know why, nor why he was not moved. But Bergljot did not tell him that virtually all other Jews in Norway had been deported to the German concentration camps.

As the war was coming to a head, and maybe approaching a crucial stage, it was important for Bergljot to place Edgar at some distance from both her and Bergen. Naturally enough in 1943 it was difficult to find people who were willing to risk their own safety by hiding a Jew. Finally she took the chance of placing him in the care of the district physician, Dr. Kari Øpstad in Fusa, further south in the county of Hordaland. This was ideal because the district had no Germans and hardly any NS-people, but also risky because Dr Øpstad was at least as involved in resistance work as Bergljot was.

Dr. Øpstad was an industrious and imperious woman. Here she is with Eir.

Kari was probably the most distinctive personality of all who helped Edgar through World War II. She obtained a medical degree in Oslo in 1923, and after a year as a candidate at Rogaland Hospital in Stavanger, she was in the municipality of Samnanger in Midhordland from 1924 to 1931. Then she ran a private practice in Sarpsborg. In 1938 she returned home to Fusa, a municipality just south of Bergen, where she became the district physician. She became a local legend as she ruled the 'Doctor Farm', a former vicarage.

Dr Øpstad - no one called her anything else - was said to have a work week of about 80 hours. Her commitment was enormous. She never hesitated to make home visits even though it was not easy to get around in the large district. During the war there was a shortage of gasoline, so one often had to improvise. In an article in 1946 about Dr Øpstad, the magazine *Bondekvinner* [Farm Women], the harsh realities were laid out in picturesque turns:

Strandviksfjorden is wide and substantial. The doctor experiences many a tough spell here when seas sweep over the little boat, so she gets wet wherever she sits down. The clothes freeze - yes, it happens sometimes she arrives, literally frozen stiff, to a farm, so that she has to stand close to an oven to thaw out before it is possible to get her coat off.

Despite her demanding job, Dr. Øpstad - who was by the way single and childless - took time for much more as well. She became involved in the temperance movement, language use (she favored the country dialect as opposed to the Norwegian used in Oslo and other cities), promoting public health education and Sunday school. In Fusa she organized the temperance lodge Senepskornet (mustard seed) for children and young people, and they held their meetings at the youth center. According to the local history book *Verda inn over dørstokken* (*The World Across Our Threshold*), Dr. Øpstad undertook over several years almost single handedly the 17 May celebrations (Norway's Constitution Day) in Fusa. She arranged for the parties in the doctoral yard, and her maid Inga Storli served homemade dravle (special gruel made with postpartum cow's milk). This was followed by the children's procession. Even in the time of the war when the celebration of the national holiday was prohibited, the efforts of the Eidsvold Fathers (Norway's Constitutional Signatories) were celebrated with the Doctor's Party at her ranch albeit in more subtle forms than customary.

Dr. Øpstad was undoubtedly fond of children in her own way, and often connected well with them as she talked to them as if they were adults. Most children like to be taken seriously and to be held accountable. At the same time she was strict and rather moralistic. Not everyone hit it off well with her, and among them was the new foster son from Bratislava and Laksevåg. Edgar felt less well in Fusa, than he had done at Laksevåg and with Bergljot Horne in Milde.

Dr.Øpstad dominated the doctoral manor totally. In addition to Edgar and Inga, two sons of the doctor's brother stayed there at this time - Ingjald and Anders. They helped in sundry ways. Ingjald Øpstad was often the driver. Anders Øpstad had an impaired leg from poliomyelitis, but was still an efficient handyman. Inga was the one who held it all together and had to face new challenges. Dr. Øpstad frequently invited guests for a spontaneous feast, often at short notice. This could appear inconsiderate during the war when there was a shortage of almost everything. But she hardly thought of it, for it was Inga who was responsible for providing food and drink.

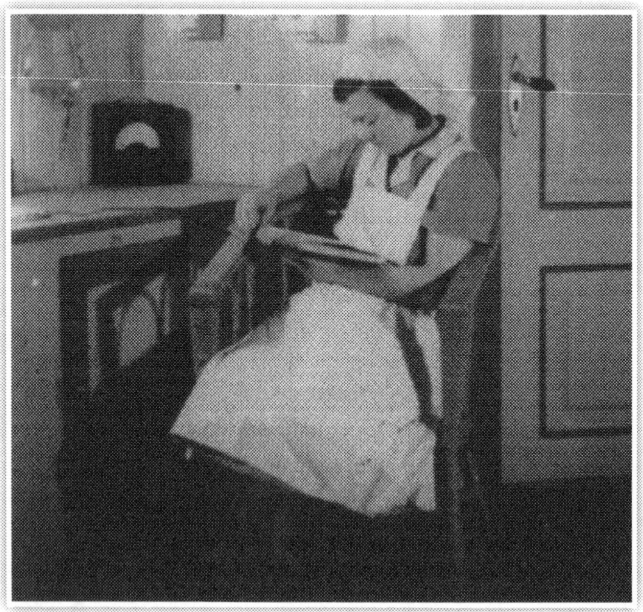

The maid Inga Storli in Fusa.

Edgar remembers the maid Inga as a simple but friendly soul, and as eminently loyal and conscientious. He often helped in the kitchen, among other things, in making starch from potatoes. Inga was as submissive as Dr. Øpstad was dominant, and it was not always fun to observe. Edgar remembers a time a lay preacher came to the farm. The preacher developed warm feelings for Inga and she reciprocated them, but in the end he went again,

leaving Inga depressed. Edgar got the impression that Dr. Øpstad had put a stop to the romance. She needed the housekeeper at the doctoral mansion.

The doctor was friendly as long as people played by her rules, but rarely accepted deviation. She had an organ with foot pedals, and got a musician to teach Edgar to play. It was hard, but Edgar was trying to learn the notes and the instrument as well as he could. After some lessons he felt encouraged to try to play a simple song his mother had taught him. If he had expected a little praise, he became disappointed.

Edgar and school friend John Storøy, sometime around 1943.

Dr. Øpstad made it clear that it sounded absolutely terrible and he got a clear message to stick to the assignment given to him by the teacher.

Edgar also remembers that he perceived U.S. President Franklin Delano Roosevelt as a hero because he had taken his country into the war, which he believed and hoped would lead to Hitler Germany's defeat. Dr. Øpstad however, had relatives in the United States and developed through them a sense of Roosevelt as the worst thing that has happened to America. Edgar was upset every time he heard Dr. Øpstad denouncing President Roosevelt while Edgar did not know enough to be able to defend him.

Another problem was that Dr. Øpstad proselytized firmly and often. Her belief in God guided her life. Everything she thought came of it. Edgar felt that his lack of devotion was not well tolerated. One of the comrades from Fusa, Johan Frøland, remember Edgar objected to both Christian teaching in the school and the foster mother's missionary urge. Edgar believes he was pragmatic. He agreed to pray for food before each meal, On other occasions, Edgar felt she went too far in her rigid outlook.

One episode has burned itself into his memory. In December 1943 Edgar and some of the other guys helped the baker in Fusa with Christmas baking. The baker was a friendly, generous and well-liked man. The boys counted cookies and put them in bags. The agreement was that if they found some that were broken or misshapen, they could eat them, or take the imperfect cookies with them. Work was consequently pleasurable and the mood high. Once on a weekend the baker indulged himself with an aquavit bottle he had standing under the counter. It gradually made him more cheerful and boisterous. He began to sing and shout. None of the boys thought it was uncomfortable. Then suddenly Dr. Øpstad stepped into the bakery. She gave the baker a major overhaul for having drunk alcohol in the presence of children. Then she confiscated the bottle. Edgar and the others felt sorry for the baker who had been humiliated in this way. The temperance movement was one of Kari Øpstad's main projects. In several interviews later in her life she chastised Christians for not daring to take the fight against alcohol seriously enough.

But Dr. Øpstad showed her tender side sometimes. Edgar will never forget his 14th birthday in February 1944, when his foster mother threw a party for him at the doctoral homestead. The highlight was when two senior members of the choir in Senepskornet lined up and sang for Edgar:

Good luck on your day Edgar,
And may you always find
a future that is bright and fine
- yes, you must win your luck.

May the bright light displace all the gloom
And evil that plagues the world.
May peace and freedom come soon
And sunshine on your journey.

To the country and people that you love the most
To father and mother and Vera
I know you long for that country
And will get to make the trip.

Yes, may you meet all
As you so often wished.
May the end soon come of this dark night
That has kept you apart.

Kari Øpstad's song had three additional stanzas, and as in the past she could not resist to preach again. But of course, the words and the two boys singing made a deep impression on Edgar.

Doctor Kari Øpstad showed her gentle traits to Edgar's liking and admiration. His favorite first rabbit,

Hanni, made an unlucky jump one day and Edgar found her limping along on three good legs and a front paw at an angle with a broken bone. Kari Øpstad was consulted and without hesitation aligned the bone. While Edgar held on to Hanni the doctor applied a small plaster cast to the rabbit's leg. Orthopedic treatment of the first class. The cast dried and firmed up rapidly and Hanni was hopping about making a tap-tap sound. Next morning Edgar found Hanni happy enough, she had chewed through the plaster cast in a straight line and did not miss it. Her leg healed properly.

Another kind deed Edgar appreciated whole heartedly was the gift from Dr. Kari Øpstad of a goat.

The year in Fusa brought greater seriousness to Edgar's life. He felt conflicted about his new home, and about the contrast to what he had felt to be a carefree existence in Laksevåg. In addition, of course, the world war proceeded. It no longer appeared harmless to Edgar. It had also been a long time since he had received a letter from his mother, father and Vera. He had not tried to send anything because he was afraid that the letters could give him or his family in Žilina problems with the Nazi authorities.

Finally even in Fusa, Germans and representatives of the Norwegian occupational authorities came to pay a visit. Edgar realized that it was wise to keep his distance. Kari, Ingjald and Anders Øpstad and most of those they knew were involved in resistance work. They had, among other things illegal radio sets, and hid resistance fighters on the run, or transported them in the doctor's car. Towards the end of the war Kari Øpstad also was in prison for a period. She later described it as pure vacation. Finally she could lie in bed for a reasonable length of time, and sleep properly in the morning.

In *Verda inn over dørstokken* [Green over the doorstep] a story is told of Dr Øpstad and Ingjald encountering a German patrol unit in Havsgårddalen while they transported someone who had escaped from German captivity in Bergen. She was driving while the two men sat in the rear seat. When the Germans stopped the car and were looking in, Ingjald was holding the fugitive's head in a firm grip while Dr. Øpstad calmly explained that this was a case of a patient with severe mental illness who had to go to the hospital as quickly as possible. The Germans let them drive on.

There were several raids on the doctor's residence, and each time Edgar was sent out by Inga or by Dr. Øpstad. They did not take his safety as lightly as his former protectors had done. Sometimes he hid up on a crag, at other times in the home of the family of Johan Frøland. During one raid Ander's copy of Karl Marx's major work *Das Kapital*, in German, was seized.

In parallel with the war's realities sinking in, Edgar also missed his mother, father, and Vera more. He had not received any letters from them since spring 1942, and assumed therefore that they might be having a hard time. Edgar thought the silence was due to the postal connection being interrupted. The whole time he was convinced that they were alive. His friend Einar Øxnevad, who lived in Bergen but spent summers in Fusa, still remembers that Edgar was worried about his family. He always had a picture of his parents and Vera in his pocket and everyone got to see it. Øxnevad also remembers one night they were on a camping trip. He heard Edgar crying after they had gone to sleep for the evening.

The boys in Fusa understood that Edgar was a refugee and without his parents, and thus it was easy to understand if his mood was not always cheerful. He was nicknamed "the Czech" although he was accurately a Slovak. In Fusa there were no children that had any knowledge of the Jews beyond what they were told in the Bible. The only thing anyone noticed out of the ordinary was that Edgar did not take off his underwear

Edgar in Fusa with his goat, 1944.

when the others stripped for a dip in the Eikelands fjord. That this could be explained by the religious tradition no one figured out until years later.

In the spring of 1944, Adolf Hitler, or at least his more temperate generals, could see the writing on the wall in all seriousness. In May, Crimea was recaptured by the Soviet Union. In the beginning of June the Western allies conquered Rome, and on the 6th of June came the massive operation Overlord, the Normandy landing. Laksevåg Mayor Arne Normann, who still had an occasional visit from his former foster son, must have felt more uncomfortable than ever.

On the other hand Edgar did not feel significantly dejected by the thought that his last year of elementary school was about to end.

He would commence in high school, at the Fana municipal public high school. Edgar took leave of Dr. Øpstad, Inga, Anders, Ingjald, his school friends, and his rabbits. Only his goat he held on to. They travelled together on the coastal ferry to Bergen where with the help of Dr. B. Horne he was able to place the goat with a farming family. After he had started in high school and got oriented to his new environment and its demands, he decided to visit his goat. Too late. The farming family had had some delicious meals leaving him only memories and sadness.

Chapter 8

"Yes, Edgar, you are different in both body and mind", the teacher told him at the Fana municipal public higher school. The new secondary school student had answered a question evidently in a somewhat unusual manner, and now his classmates stared. Nothing else happened, but Edgar got another reminder that he was not like everyone else, even though he long ago spoke flawless Norwegian.

The war went into the bloody final stages. Although Edgar never experienced the most serious war events in the Bergen area at close range, he got more than enough taste of misery. He constantly heard bangs and saw flames and worried about Arne and Agnes, and friends in Bergen. At a safe distance in Fana he saw and heard in October 1944, the Allied bombing of Laksevåg including Holen school where 60 students were killed. Together with a friend who had also gone to Holen school, he went into Laksevåg to see the devastation, and ensure that Agnes and Arne were safe.

This year also meant yet another change of environment. From Dr. Øpstad's strict regime in Fusa, Edgar returned to Fana and the far more liberal Dr. Horne. But this time he would not stay with Bergljot. First, Edgar was accommodated for a period of time in the big house of the family Eikeland, a widow and her three grown sons. The eldest had been a sailor and could tell stories from far away. The middle one lived in the house with his wife and a boxer dog. The youngest was newly engaged, very lively and with a penchant for daring jokes and other antics. One of his favorites was to light his own fart with matches. Edgar got to experience how it caught fire and the boy got lighter burns back there. In this family, Edgar also learned to play poker, which Dr. Øpstad in Fusa strongly disliked. While he lived with the Eikeland family, Edgar began at the Fana municipal public higher education. On his way to and from school on his bicycle he passed Trollhaugen the residence of the no longer living composer Edward Grieg.

After some pleasant months, the youngest Eikeland son Erling was getting married. The family needed the extra room that Edgar occupied. Edgar was moved to the Elverhøy boarding house in Nesttun. Here Edgar for the first time experienced living independently. He was given a room on the top floor. Maybe this room was not officially a guest room, because the only other person who lived in another small room on that floor was the hired maid of the establishment.

Bergljot Horne continued to hold his passport, but kept slack rein. Now Edgar began to be grownup and independent.

In the boardinghouse, he became familiar with other residents. A nice man took Edgar to the racetrack for the first time. Others taught him how to play bridge. While living at the Elverhøy boardinghouse, Edgar remembers that he read works by Henrik Ibsen.

In his room he fastened a large map of Europe on the wall After scanning each day's newspaper he was able to highlighted the front with red and blue flags. The Nazi-controlled media reported that the ever-victorious German forces had inflicted heavy casualties on their enemies in given locations. With a glance at the map, Edgar could ascertain that it really was a German retreat. He moved the red

Eastern flags westwards and the blue Allied flags eastwards according to the names listed in the published communiques.

Ever since he heard that the United States entered the war on the Allied side in1942, Edgar had thought that the Germans would lose in the end. Now he realized from the published locations of the battles that the turning point had arrived. Soon there was no doubt - the war was nearing its end.

Edgar's friend from Fusa, Johan Frøland, remembers that in the autumn of 1944 he went one weekend to Bergen to visit family. Edgar came also to visit with his former foster parents in Nygårdsvik. Arne Normann had begun as director of Bergen Tramways, while the Laksevåg municipal administration was merged with that of Bergen where NS-mayor Alf Johannessen was to administer the combined districts. Johan and Edgar took a city tour after dark. Despite the absence of street lights, it was pretty crowded at Torgallmenningen. Suddenly there was a bang. Probably someone had fired a firecracker to liven up the atmosphere. German soldiers moved in with dogs and flashlights. Shortly after Johan and Edgar stood, each with a light beam in his face, and had to explain that neither of them was responsible for the blast. The soldiers moved on. Johan did not seem to be affected by the incident, but remembers that Edgar became nervous, "Come on, let's go", he said.

Peace would in a way be the start of Edgar's war, but he did not know this when General Alfred Jodl signed the Third Reich's capitulation on May 7, 1945. Sensational and encouraging messages from the Continent had also reached western Norway for weeks. Hitler was dead. Goebbels was dead. But although the Nazi power machine's joints were creaking, it held up pretty well until much later in the evening of May 7th when even the most skeptical dared to believe that the war was over. Then the blackout was lifted in Bergen, and the lights came on the day after peace was formally declared in Norway. Elverhøy house erupted in wild celebration, but what Edgar remembers most was all the aggressive verbal attacks against the Germans and the Norwegian National Socialists. Of course he was long aware of how the fronts moved, and that Arne Normann stood on the wrong side. But only now did he realize how serious the problem Arne and Agnes would end up in. Edgar's mind was divided. Partly it was in Nygårdsvik, but primarily it was in Žilina. Now he had to immediately connect with his parents and go to them. The last letter from home he had was in spring 1942. Edgar thought the reason was that the Nazis had broken mail communications, but now that the war was over shouldn't they be repaired?

The letter was sent to Žilina May 12, and Edgar wrote in English. The reason was probably that his mother had complained so much about his German already in 1942, and he had not been very diligent in maintaining the language in the years since. Besides, he might impress by showing that he could now also manage the use of world language, English.

> My dear parents and sister. I congratulate with the peace, and hope that you have it very good. If possible, you must send a letter. Mr. Normann is arrested because he was "Nazi". I am going in the first class of the highest grade school. I hope you can understand my English. I am most eager to depart for home. My cordial greetings to all of you at home. Love from Edgar.

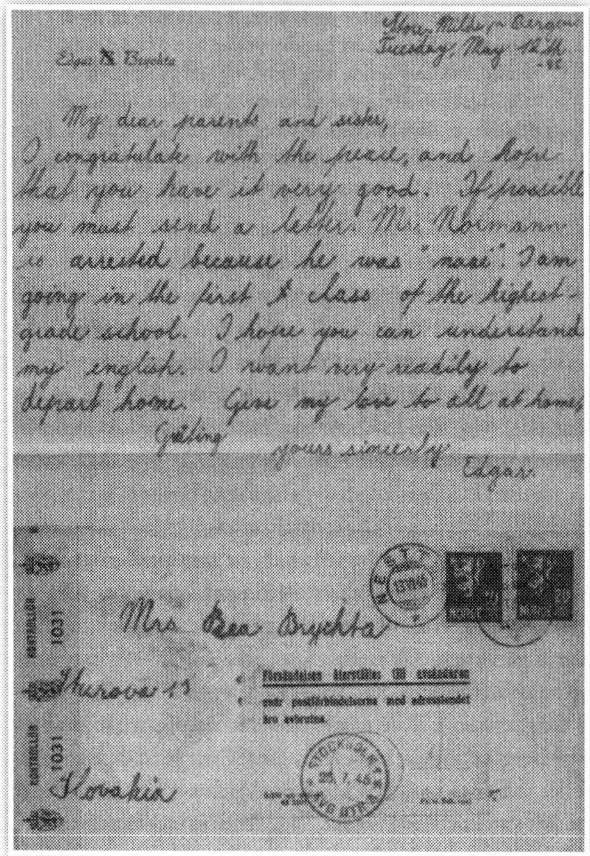

Tuesday, May 12th -45

My dear parents and sister,
I congratulate with the peace, and hope that you have it very good. If possible you must send a letter. Mr. Normann is arrested because he was "nazi". I am going in the first class of the highest grade school. I hope you can understand my english. I want very readily to depart home. Give my love to all at home.

yours sincerely
Edgar.

Mrs Bea Brychta
1031
1031
Slovakia

The letter Edgar sent to his parents and sister on 12 May 1945.

Now began a long and frustrating wait. Would the letter arrive at Žilina? Would the answer find the road up to the boarding house Elverhøy in Nesttun? Nothing else was on Edgar's mind during this time, and therefore he remembers little else of what happened in the Norwegian peacetime. That his mother, father and Vera would not be alive, was not a thought that had struck him. Gas chambers, he had not heard about yet. But what had Edgar really thought about his parents and sister while the war was ongoing? The fact that contact via letters had stopped created uncertainty, but it was put in mental parentheses. There was nothing he could do while the war was in progress, and life had to go on. When peace came, the parentheses were removed. Missing them was intense.

Edgar cannot remember when he had the first contact with Bergljot Horne and her son George in the early days of peace. Nor whether he spoke with Agnes and Arne Normann. Everything was chaos within Norway's land. He remembers that he was in the city center and saw the 17 May parade, the Norwegians first real celebration of their constitution, a national holiday, since 1939. Edgar could have participated in the procession, under three sections: The Fana municipal public higher education, in the Scouts that had been banned during the war, and also the section in which the foreigners who found themselves in Bergen when peace was declared. However, he remained among the spectators. His joy was more cautious.

Another of the few tangible memories of the Norwegian spring was that he became acquainted with a family from Troms, a distant part in the north of Norway, which they had been forced to leave. They landed in Elverhøy. They invited Edgar for a trip to Rundemanen and Ulrikken, popular mountaintops enjoyed by natives and visitors.

The trip was fine. It was the weekend of the change of currency from wartime paper tender to the new banknotes with the King's and the legitimately elected government's guarantee. The wartime paper money was without value and the new bills would not be issued until the following Monday. Coins however were still allowed as legal tender. Edgar had saved coins in order to buy gifts for his parents and sister Vera, With a pocket heavy with his coins he became the banker of the day and was able to proudly finance the refreshment at the restaurant. The next day he also felt rich as he was reimbursed with crisp newly issued paper currency worth considerably more than the heavy content of his pants pocket the prior day.

Edgar also remembers another episode at the end of May 1945. Bergljot Horne was told that the Gestapo had left her home and medical offices in Store Markevei, and that she could come back. Edgar and George got to be with her when she went there. Disappointed, but certainly not particularly surprised, they found that the apartment was upside down and half destroyed. The Germans had obviously departed thoroughly frustrated. On the wall hung a large portrait of Adolf Hitler, with five or six bullet holes through his forehead and through the wall behind.

Arne Normann was reported to the police already on 8 May, the day following the capitulation of the Third Reich. The following day he was arrested. On the 10th of May he was sent to the Espeland prison camp. This hardly came as a surprise to either Arne or Agnes. Maybe they even felt relief. The last months of the war had not been a good time for them. As Germany's impending defeat became obvious, people felt themselves freer to retaliate against - or have revenge upon - their oppressors. Several years later, when Arne finally lifted the veil for his adopted daughter Anne, she learned a bit about how things had turned out. Sometime towards the

Arne Normann was arrested May 9, 1945, on suspicion of treason. (Photo: Bergen City Archives and the Archives of Resistance.)

end of the war, when Arne was walking in Laksevåg, a group of men come after him. At least one of them had a weapon. Arne was sure that his last hour had come, but tried to outrun them. He managed to turn a corner and jump down into a cellar vault, where he hid and heard his pursuers run past. If he had not known this neighborhood like the back of his hand, he would have been dead, said Arne. Soon after, a similar situation arose and this time Arne was saved by a man - perhaps another member of the N.S. party - who happened to drive along and let him jump inside his vehicle.

Although Agnes was not as exposed, everyone knew she was not a member of the N.S. party, she naturally felt she should not remain living alone in Nygårdsvik. She took little Anne first to some relatives in Kvam in the valley of Gudbrandsdalen, later to her family in Nordfjordeid.

During the summer of 1945, Arne's mother became seriously ill in her home in Stokmarknes. He was granted three weeks leave to visit her, and while on leave, also visited Agnes in Nordfjodeid. On the return home, he sent a postcard to Edgar:

> Dear Edgar. I am now on my way back to Bergen, just passing Måløy. My mother died two days after I got home, and I'm happy that I got the chance to see and talk with her before she died. I sent you a camera and hope that you've received it. Dad would have liked to have you take a trip up north and you may hear from him about it. Agnes received your letter while I was there. You are wished all the best Edgar from Arne.

George and Edgar at Bergljot's residence in Store Markevei 4b. Inside the residence was partially destroyed.

The card, dated July 9th, contained not a word about detention or treason or anything that had to do with the war. Perhaps it was a condition of his leave, maybe he would not take up such issues with Edgar. A second post card from Arne, dated July 14, in the nature of being a post script, and perhaps also of being a somewhat sentimental request:

> Along the way on the train I suddenly remembered that I should have informed you that I have packed the tent you were talking about to let you have it. Luckily, I placed it in the hall with a label, and let Mrs. Ytterhorn know that you will fetch it there. Unfortunately I forgot to also inform you as well. Tent poles are wrapped inside the canvas. One pole may be missing, but you can easily make a new one. Hope you have many a nice trip with the tent in the woods and meadows this summer. Arne.

The letter-card had the postal stamp of Nesttun as Arne Normann probably travelled to Elverhøy boarding house in order to visit Edgar but did not find him at home. Although Arne did not comment on his incarceration, it is implicit in the letter that he will not be home. This suggests that at least he is aware that Edgar understands the situation. In the end of July, Edgar's letter to his parents was returned via Stockholm. "Försändelsen återställes till avsändaren enär postförbindelserna med adresslandet äro avbrutna" [The mailing is being returned to the sender because the postal connection with the country of destination is interrupted] was printed on a pasted on label.

Edgar and a family from Troms touring Rundemanen.

After waiting for so long, this was frustrating for Edgar. The message that it was not possible to send mail to Slovakia did not elucidate anything.

Edgar now had to try to work things out in other ways. His maternal grandfather had six daughters, three with his first wife who died shortly after she had her third daughter. Than the widower grandfather married again and with his second wife had another three daughters. The eldest of these six maternal aunts of Edgar died of Hodgkin's disease before Edgar was born. His mother Regina (Rea for short) was the second of the first three daughters. The last one of these first three, Ernestina (Erna) had started work in England as an au pair with an affluent British family before the outbreak of the war. The address Edgar had for Ernestina was no longer her current one. The British postal service nevertheless was able to deliver the letter from Edgar to her new location. She had married a chemical engineer originally from Poland. Together they emigrated to Canada where years later Edgar, his wife Judy and their children visited them. Of the three younger aunts, Rea's half sisters, the eldest Liese had slipped out of Czechoslovakia with the last train before the borders were virtually closed. Liese spent the war years in England working for an organization providing care for disabled and homeless service personnel. After the armistice she returned to her hometown, Chomutov, in Czechoslovakia. Fritzi the middle of Rea's half sisters escaped from Czechoslovakia with her husband, an operatic singer. They ended up in Canada. Edgar's youngest aunt, Edith (Didi) also escaped from Czechoslovakia in the nick of time. She came to England where she got training as a nurse and midwife. Edgar had her address and hoped that she was still there. Although she had in the meantime moved to another place in England, the postal service ensured that Edgar's letter would arrive. In answer to his letter, his aunt told him that she knew nothing about what had happened with Rea, Max and Vera. But she sent the addresses of her sisters.

Liese, the only one of Edgar's relatives who was again living in Czechoslovakia in 1946 became Edgar's contact point in the effort to find out what had happened.

Edgar sent letters to Liese, and got a response that she also knew nothing about his parents, but she could not imagine that they were alive. Edgar, however, was welcome to come and stay with her if he wanted to look for them. Chomutov lies entirely in the northwest, on the border with Germany, and was therefore not a perfect base for Edgar. He wanted first and foremost to look where his family had lived: Bratislava, Žilina and Český T☒šin. Liese's invitation was still welcome, and a necessary stepping stone.

Now, late in the fall of 1945, Edgar and Bergljot began making concrete plans for his return home. At this time it was not just necessary to bring your passport and board a plane. Many letters had to be sent, and permits obtained.

Arne sat imprisoned waiting for his case to come up, but Edgar had letter contact with Agnes in Nordfjordeid. She told Edgar how he could visit Arne, but for reasons unknown he never went to the prison for a visit. However, Edgar traveled for Christmas to Stokmarknes to visit Arne's brother and his wife. Arne's father had died earlier in the autumn, just shortly after he became a widower. Edgar spent much of Christmas admiring the enchanted twilight of northern Norway outside and reading Cervantes' great work *Don Quixote* inside.

Gradually the bureaucratic pieces fell in place, and the journey to Chomutov approached. He was only 16 on February 5, 1946. It was celebrated at the home of Bergljot, George and Harry. Harry had come back from his exile on the other side of the North Sea. Edgar had contracted jaundice - Hepatitis A - and was not able to eat his birthday cake. But he was put in a room next door to Bergljot's medical office, and the combination of continuous medical assistance and good care led to his rapid recovery.

Shortly after, Edgar went by train to Oslo to receive the latest permissions from the legation of the reunited Czechoslovakia, and from the Norwegian agency for prisoner and refugee issues. This office was under the Ministry of Social Affairs, and was responsible for returning Norwegian political prisoners from Germany, for Germans in Norway that were to be sent home, and also for Jewish refugees. Edgar came to Oslo with the afternoon train. The Czechoslovak legation had promised to meet him and arrange accommodation for the night, but did not fulfill its promise. Edgar had to use almost all the money he had for a hotel room. After some searching in the streets around Østbanestasjonen, he found the now defunct Hotel d'Angleterre, and checked in there. Edgar was not familiar with either large buildings or luxury, so it did not take much to impress him. The d'Angleterre was fun. In a subsequent letter, Bergljot complimented him for his good taste, she had even stayed at this hotel once. However, she was not thrilled with the Czechoslovak embassy who had not arranged for accommodation as promised. Edgar ought to use his savings on completely different things than on expensive hotel rooms.

The next day, Edgar obtained the required permission to leave Norway and return to Czechoslovakia. But first Edgar had to answer searching questions: Did he really want to travel from Norway to the insecure

Central Europe now that he lacked only a year to complete high school? Edgar was admonished that it was an important decision to return home, he would abandon his residence permit in Norway. The Norwegian functionary even offered to provide a place to stay so Edgar could attend a local school while also obtaining more definitive news about his family.

But Edgar made it crystal clear that he was going home to find his family, and later that day he sat on a plane for the first time, a German Ju-52 that the Czech airline CSA had taken over after the war. The journey took him first to Copenhagen where some passengers were added for the flight to Prague.

In October 1939 he had set off from Bratislava on a train with the destination Oslo.

Now, 1946, he was back in Czechoslovakia. Viewed this way the circle was complete.

Chapter 9

As the capital of the Protectorate of Bohemia and Moravia, Prague was bombed by the Allies toward the end of the war. Among other things important buildings in the city's beautiful historic center were lost. But it was far from the carpet bombing many German cities were exposed to at this stage, nor anywhere near the Allied bombing of Laksevåg that Edgar had seen the results of up close. The returning refugee had therefore no strong sense of the horrors of war when he first returned to central Europe. In Prague, Edgar was greeted by an old friend of Aunt Liese, who accompanied him to Chomutov on a train in the northwesterly direction.

Before the war, Chomutov, located near the border of Germany, had about 33,000 inhabitants. The great majority were ethnic Germans. Czechs and Jews made up only small minorities. The city was therefore seen as Hitler-friendly before and during the war. Two large factories - Mannesmann producing among other things weapons, and Poldi steel - were contributing to the German war industry. Therefore, the city became a natural bombing target of the Allies. A massive action took place the same day in Prague. 3,400 bombs fell, destroying factories, the railway station and many other buildings. But not even in Chomutov were the results of the bombing mission visually obtrusive. The city's industrial area was not close to the main residential district.

Additionally in February 1946, as a result of the so-called Beneš decrees, Chomutov had been almost cleared of the largest segment of its population. Edvard Beneš, who was deposed when the Germans took over in 1939, had during the war led the government in exile from London. They prepared for the aftermath of the war by adopting a series of decrees - which were then implemented. The most famous and controversial stated that Hungarians and Germans would lose their property and citizenship in the reunited Czechoslovakia. When peace came it was particularly Germans who were driven out with great determination, and many were also killed in retaliation. Until November 1, 1946, some 1.5 million Germans were expelled. 3,000 villages and towns were downright depopulated before the Czechs later came and settled in many of them.

Edgar experienced the tail end of this process. As he took a walk in the woods one of the first days after his arrival in Chomutov, he met two men. One carried a rifle. The other had a white ribbon on his arm. The armed man asked Edgar where he was going. Edgar said he was getting reacquainted with the area and was walking by himself. Edgar had not heard or spoken Czech nor Slovak for the last seven years. He had years of German classes in Norwegian schools and it having been the first language of his childhood, he answered in German. The man with the rifle sounded aggressive as he asked: "Where is your armband? As a German you should have a white band on your arm!" Edgar explained his situation as a returned Slovak Jew. He also showed the new identification paper he had received. This resolved the problem and the two men went on their way.

The time at Aunt Liese's was frustrating. Edgar remembered almost no Slovak, and could not find a job. That he still knew German was not of great help at that time. Additionally, nobody knew anything about his parents and sister. Every time he asked someone, he received mostly just sad and pitying facial expressions in response. Some also gave discouraging descriptions about what had happened to Jews they had known. Edgar at 16 was realistic enough to realize that his family had probably been affected by the same disaster. Yet he did not quite give up hope of finding them alive. Above all, he could not believe that Vera, who would now be 11 years old, was dead.

Edgar maintained contact with Norway, especially Bergljot Horne and her son George. No letter from either Agnes nor Arne was found in Edgar's collection of mail from this period in Czechoslovakia, but he remembers that he corresponded at least with Agnes. A letter from Harald, Agnes' brother in Nordfjordeid, was preserved. It is dated 15 June 1946, was sent to Bergljot Horne's address, and forwarded by her.

Harald wished Edgar luck with the journey home and sent 20 crown from him and from his father 'Old Jakub' to help out. This money Bergljot put into a Norwegian bank account for Edgar. Harald also wondered what was happening to the legal proceedings for treason against Arne. The former foster father was at this time imprisoned, but his case had not come to trial yet. Agnes had secured a position as a house keeper and had Anne there with her.

Harald sent greetings from some acquaintances of Edgar's in Nordfjordeid. Clearly there were some, known to Harald, who had leanings in directions they ought to have avoided during the war time.

> Greetings from NN (the author's anonymization); you know he was of the ones involved with sundry things during the time of the war. But he has remained free most of the time since the capitulation of Germany. His case has not been heard in court yet.

A letter from one of Edgar's aunts and her husband in Canada came also via Bergljot. The two thought it was an extremely bad idea that Edgar return home to Czechoslovakia. He ought to come to them in Canada, or to another relative in the United States. They offered to help with the bureaucratic formalities and arrange financial support from other relatives.

Edgar must have accepted the offer, or have thought of saying yes, as he sent a letter to Bergljot about the matter. In a reply dated July 11, 1946 she supported his decision fully:

> I'm so glad because I know you are going to travel to Canada or the USA. There are future opportunities, especially for a clever and gifted boy like you.

Bergljot also told him that she had sent a package down to Chomutov. Unfortunately, she could not obtain more sardines than the few she had left at home, but she promised to send more, and more cod liver oil, in August. And did he have the clothes he would need in the autumn?

Edgar quickly dropped the idea of America. He had to continue the search especially in the cities where his family had lived - Bratislava, Česky Těšín and Žilina. But all three were far from Chomutov, and it was difficult to get around initially after the war. Neither Edgar nor Liese had money. He had heard of a Jewish orphanage in Prague. It now also offered shelter for young refugees. Since he did not feel it helpful to remain in Chomutov, he decided in late summer 1946 to go to the capital, which was close enough for him to reach.

He said goodbye to Liese, who had opened her doors to him. Edgar was never properly acquainted with her during this hectic period. But later in life he came in contact with her children, then adults, who told him she was a very independent woman. Liese was already a Communist in her youth. During her exile in London during the war, she was politically active and also had a son out of wedlock. The Communist conviction Liese retained even after the war. In all, she was something of a black sheep in the large and otherwise politically conservative Jewish family.

Shortly after Edgar had left Chomutov, she moved away from there - in protest against Czechoslovakia's conduct towards its German population after the war. She was upset that all her non-Jewish

German friends were forced out of the country, including Communists and others who had stood in opposition to the Nazis. Liese moved to Germany, where she married a German man, and had a daughter with him. The marriage was happy, but rested on an assumption that suddenly changed. Liese's husband, certain that he was a widower, had been lead to believe that his first wife had succumbed during the war. Suddenly the woman reappeared. This resulted in Liese's marriage being annulled. One day, her 7-year-old son Peter came home from school; he could smell gas before he saw his mother, dead, with her head in the oven.

Edgar took the train from Chomutov to Prague. Arriving at the orphanage, it was probably in August 1946, Edgar was accepted as a resident. Again he tried to do his search by contacting various offices and organizations, but without success. He also found a relative of his, a tailor Frantisek Maxa, who had married a Christian Czech lady before the war and was hidden by her family. This man also knew nothing about what had happened to Max, Rea and Vera.

The director of the orphanage lent Edgar an English book. The idea was that Edgar would benefit greatly from learning the world language properly. The director also held out the promise of helping Edgar to get accepted at Charles University in Prague. The alternative would have been to concentrate on Czech, but the orphanage director had a hunch that Edgar would not be settling down in Czechoslovakia for the long term. Edgar read English, and was open to eventually studying in Prague.

At the Jewish shelter in Prague he met a married couple acting as counselors for the young residents. Both were attracted by the blond boy who looked younger than he was. They began to get involved in his life. Edgar seems to remember that they had lost a son in the war. Perhaps this contributed to their interest.

The couple were avid supporters of Zionism, i.e. the notion that Jews constitute a nation with an historical right to Palestine. They began to recruit Edgar also for the cause, and with such enthusiasm that they advised against him spending time on English. They thought it was far more important to learn the Zionist ideology and Hebrew. They belonged to the branch of Zionists called Hashomer Hazair, a left leaning group eager to bring able bodied members to their ranks for the journey to Palestine and the destined state of Israel. They set out to recruit Edgar.

Palestine after World War I was a British mandate, established by the UN's predecessor the League of Nations, with the purpose of giving the Jews a national home. In the 1920s, approximately 100,000 Jews moved to Palestine. Tel Aviv grew as a Hebrew speaking city. Initially the migration elicited no great Arabic resistance, but this changed gradually as the numbers of immigrating Jews increased. In 1929, Arab groups conducted a pogrom in Hebron and killed 67 Jews. Hebron had been home to Jewish settlers for centuries. By 1936, there were 400,000 Jews in Palestine, mostly refugees from the growing Nazism in Germany. The same year, there was a large wave of Arab opposition against Jewish immigration. This caused increasing clashes between Jewish and Arab armed groups. Britain holding the power of the mandate responded by imposing restrictions on immigration. Many Jewish refugees from Europe were placed in refugee camps in other countries. This lead to illegal immigration both during and after the war. Armed Jewish groups conducted several attacks on the British. In 1946 King David Hotel in Jerusalem, where many British service men were staying, was blown up and 92 people were killed.

The Zionist couple, Berci and Miriam Bornstein, thought Edgar might acknowledge that his family had perished in the extermination camps, and that it was better for him to turn away from Europe. Edgar was reluctant to go to the Middle East. He had been leaning towards going in the opposite direction. On the other hand, Edgar developed a certain sympathy for Zionism. Perhaps those were right who claimed that Jews could only be safe in a country of their own? The journey to Palestine would be a new adventure, a new step into the unknown. After gaining some knowledge of Edgar's interests, the zealous recruiters could also highlight the kibbutz, the Jewish agricultural commune, as a tempting opportunity. Finally, Edgar said yes.

To increase the chances that the exodus would succeed, Edgar got an expedited issue of false identity papers. He kept his own image, but got a new name and age: 18 - even though he was only 16 and looked like he was 14. The Bornsteins, wasted no time. As soon as the paperwork was on hand, Edgar was ready for the train ride to Marseille or LeHavre, there to board a ship aiming for Palestine. It was not expected that the ship would reach the shore of this land. The waters were patrolled by British war ships ready to divert any ship carrying Jews wanting to settle in Palestine without permission from the British authorities exerting their League of Nations-agreed-upon mandate over Palestine. The passenger ships were routed to Cypress where their human cargo was placed in refugee camps supervised by the British. Edgar was aware of this. A period in British captivity on Cyprus would mean even more adventure. Monday August 18, 1946 Edgar was put on a train for France. From there a ship would take him and the other hopefuls to Palestine. The Bornstein couple stood on the platform in Prague and waved him goodbye.

Just when the train was ready to move Edgar pulled the emergency brake, grabbed his suitcase and aimed for the exit. He does not recall details, maybe he had a disagreement with someone. He certainly felt he was giving up his last opportunity to find traces of his family. He was most certain still that his sister was alive and that he could find her and help her in her life. "What are you doing?" someone shouted after him, as Edgar moved over the tracks back to the Bornstein couple. They were mildly surprised, but they collected themselves and went with Edgar back to the Jewish orphanage.

The couple remained steadfast in their resolution. In just a few days they arranged space for Edgar in a residential setting for Jewish youth operated by the organization, Hashomer Hatzair. This time Edgar was easily persuaded as the suggested facility was situated in Bratislava. There he felt his chances of finding traces of his family were promising.

He remembered the location of the building where the family had lived before moving to Žilina. Also his school Hodzova Skola he found with ease. Ludmila Raiova had taken care of him and Vera while the parents were working. He did not succeed in locating her after some 11 years of separation. Renka Lieferantova, wife of the janitor in the building where the Brichta family had rented an apartment, was still in Bratislava. Her husband had succumbed during the war, but their son, Edgar's friend, Fredy (Alfred) lived. Just before Edgar found Mrs. Renka Lieferant, Fredy, under the auspices of a Zionist organization, had emigrated to Israel where he became a tractor operator on a kibbutz.

In Bratislava, Edgar went to the municipal offices and got a copy of his birth certificate. He would surely need it. He again contacted various organizations and government agencies to find out something about the Brichta family.

In a letter to Bergljot and George, Edgar wrote that he had been in a camp, but his stay there was supposed to bring him on to Palestine. Bergljot replied September 20, obviously disappointed that nothing came of either the U.S. or Canada plans.

> Dear Edgar! Just got home from the East (of Norway) and found your letter and cards. Both George and I were so worried over your move to a Zionist facility. Will you be there long? Be kind and reply as soon as possible and let me know if I can send you a package?

So Edgar sent a letter to Bergen, this time only to George. He and George's mother responded in separate letters dated October 20, 1946:

> Many thanks for the letter, Edgar! I've been so worried for you this summer, so I have to say that your letter was very welcome. When you wrote to George that you were in Bratislava, I did not really know what I should believe, as I did not get permission to read any of the letter, you see.

Bergljot asked to be thoroughly updated immediately, offered him more sardines, and regretted that it was so difficult to send out sweets - she could still keep hiding some candies in bags of oatmeal, which he probably still enjoyed. Bergljot also sent greetings from her friend and colleague Dr. Øpstad, who had been on a trip to Denmark. In his letter, George updated Edgar on the situation at school and the teachers they both had had - one of them had suddenly begun to cry in front of the class, and "the hippo has not improved!" This time Edgar mentioned that he intended to travel to Palestine one day.

> ARE YOU going to Palestine? Is it bombed much where you are now? When will you travel to Palestine?

Specific questions about Palestine were probably more than Edgar could answer. He was in the house administered by Hashomer Hazair and tried to fit in as best he could. Physical training and education in Jewish history and Hebrew was the order of the day. Edgar tried to secure title to any property his parents' might be entitled. Lack of support from the bureaucracy led to no progress. In one letter he also mentioned that work assignments took up much of their time. The response from Bergen dated December 7, 1946 mentioned that Bergljot had had a hospital stay, and regretted the late reply:

> It sounds like there is tremendous pressure of work in your organization. I think it's horribly unjust that other people should have more control over your parents' and grandparents' property than you who is heir. I think you should stand by your rights. I do Edgar.

Aunt Bergljot, as she had called herself in the last letter, was clearly concerned that the plan about Palestine still existed, and hinted further:

> You never mentioned any more about that letter from Canada. Was it so utterly impossible then?

Edgar settled in a bit, and was in Hashomer Hatzair throughout all of 1947. He was asked what work he could do, and answered that he wanted to become a fisherman. He had in fact done some recreational fishing in Norway. The leaders replied that there were not so many fish in the Danube. He was sent to a furniture factory, where the task was to polish furniture. After a few weeks of manually polishing assorted furniture, Edgar had had enough and said thanks, but no thanks.

One day Edgar got an unexpected visit at the group home by a relative on his mother's side. She was now living in Palestine, where she was also politically active. She had been attending a conference in Switzerland. In one way or another, perhaps through American relatives, she had heard that Edgar was in Bratislava. She also had discovered that Edgar liked sweets, and brought a box of Swiss chocolates. They talked for a while, and Edgar confided to her that his heart was not entirely with Zionism. Then they agreed that it was probably better to focus on North America again. But he should stay with Hashomer Hatzair for the time being.

Eventually Edgar was moved from the group home in Bratislava, which was intended for younger members, to a group home for older members 18 and up, in Kosice in the eastern part of the country. The departure to Palestine was constantly postponed because of the turmoil there. In a letter to Bergljot when he mentioned America again, she responded enthusiastically on 16 April 1947:

> I became so glad for your last letter where you talk about America. I wish something would materialize with this. America is where the great opportunities are. Palestine I think is becoming more and more problematic. Central Europe also, even though the country of Czechoslovakia seems best.

And again she promised to smuggle more sweets in oatmeal, and to submit a new Norwegian stamp series to Edgar's collection. Correspondence with George went separately, and George had obviously had a mysterious mission in Fusa from Edgar. In a letter dated September 9th, he wrote that he was there in July: "I looked everywhere for you know what, but I found none".

An additional letter from Bergljot September 25, 1947 shows that she held the iron to the fire as a dedicated 'aunt'. She read much about how bad the conditions were in Central Europe, certainly a new prod to encourage Edgar to make the move to America.

As time went by in Kosice, Edgar became more and more impatient. The Zionists continually spoke of there being an imminent departure for Palestine. But the turmoil around what would be the creation of Israel did not cease. Edgar was still not convinced that he wanted to go. Moreover, he felt that he hadn't learned much of benefit for his future. His own family's fate remained unclear. He had not yet had the opportunity to visit Žilina, the last city where he knew they had lived.

In a letter to Bergljot, he asked for advice. She answered October 29 as best she could: "It is obvious that you cannot go with the others to Palestine when everything is as it is." She thought it was sad that Edgar did not learn anything of significance, but urged him to at least learn Czech well. She imagined that there could be opportunities in the diplomatic service. Moreover Bergljot deplored another event:

> Here in Norway there are large collections all over for Yugoslavia and Romania, and probably to Germany. But the last they dare not post, because it would be bad propaganda. Can you comprehend why countries with as rich and fertile soil as Hungary and Romania should require the sending of flour and bread from Norway which is all rocks?

That Norway would send fish and cod liver oil, Bergljot found to be more reasonable, she wrote. She herself supplied this to Edgar.

While being a member of the Zionist group home in Kosice, Edgar worked in the autumn of 1947 first as a delivery boy and general helper for a Jewish wholesale millinery and a tailoring supply business in Kosice. Later he became a delivery boy for a Jewish grocer's store. Using a bicycle equipped with a basket, he delivered groceries to customers. According to a letter from George, Edgar also toyed with the idea of becoming an English teacher. Besides the thoughts about America and Palestine, another idea cropped up in Edgar's head. How about returning to Norway?

On advice from his relatives in Canada and USA, Edgar made contact with the American Joint Distribution Committee (AJDC), a Jewish self help organization that since 1914 had worked for needy and homeless Jews.

AJDC was among other projects heavily involved in the emigration to Palestine. In the autumn of 1947 AJDCs office in Bratislava helped Edgar to consider his options and decide what to do next in life. In a letter from AJDC Bratislava to AJDC Oslo on January 15, 1948, there appears mention of Edgar and the personnel of the organization had tried to find a way for him to enter the USA. Even if his relatives were willing to assist, he would "not be able to get a visa for many years". Additional interviews with the 17-year-old, however, shed light on a good alternative approach.

> He has now definitely decided that he would go back to Norway, where he said he had been extremely happy. Our personal interviews with the boy have convinced us that this would be the best solution for him.

In the letter it was also stated that Edgar had been promised a visa by the Norwegian consul in Prague, while AJDC now helped him to obtain a passport. The question to AJDC Oslo was whether they could contact those who had cared for him in Norway to find out if someone was willing to take him back - until he reached the age of consent, 21. This was a requirement that Norwegian authorities asked to enable Edgar to return. Meanwhile AJDC Bratislava would contact their people in New York to clarify whether Edgar's American relatives could help to fund further study or training.

Probably Edgar did not know that AJDC worked at this time to specifically get him another move to Norway; for a time in January 1948 he resumed contact by letter with Arild Birkeli in Nygårdsvik without mentioning the thought of moving back. Instead, he asked his buddy from the war, which he remembered was leftist, for the Norwegian version of The International [a world famous song in the labor movement, used by Russia as the Soviet Union anthem until 1944]. Arild, now active and engaged with young Communists, wrote with delight the text for the song, and sent it by letter.

> Of course I am terribly glad to hear that you are a Marxist, but you should know that you are my friend regardless of any political affiliation you may have.

Edgar had not been much of a Marxist, but still tried to adapt to the environment, i.e. the red Zionists. He had written to Arild, who he remembered was left-wing, and asked for the text because he constantly heard the International sung in Hebrew in the camp in Kosice without understanding a word. Studies in Hebrew thus had not shed much light on the meaning of the song.

How long it was since they last had contact, Arild showed in another paragraph of a letter dated 29 January 1948:

> You must greet your parents for me and say that here in Norway we respect Czechoslovakia for their solidarity and the fervor they show for the reconstruction of their country, and at least for a new and better world.

In Norway AJDC was represented by the head of the Jewish Social Committee in Oslo, Marcus Levin, who also headed The Mosaic Religious Community. His secretary there, Josef Berg, quickly learned in turn to follow up the request from Bratislava. On the 4th

of February, he sent identical letters to "Mr. Dr. K. Opstad", "Mr. Engineer Normann" and "Mr. Dr. B. Horne".

> From Bratislava, we have received notification that your previous foster son, Edgar Brichta, born 05/02/1930, wants to return to Norway. Our connection in Bratislava thinks this would be the best solution for him as his attempt to reach the United States has been in vain. Efforts are currently under way to provide him with passports and visas to Norway.
>
> As the authorities here demand to know if there are any in this country who are willing to take care of him, we therefore dare ask you to inform us whether you are willing to help the boy, at least initially. We would be grateful to you for your speedy response.

A speedy reply came from Fusa, where Kari Øpstad sent the letter back February 9 with the following inscription:

> Response to The Jewish Social Committee. Unfortunately I cannot do anything for Edgar Brichta. When he traveled from here, I had to choose between letting the housekeeper go or letting the boy journey. And should I take him back, she would surely go at once. Sincerely, K. Øpstad.

This message was obviously not meant for Edgar's eyes, but he was surprised when he saw it many years later. He traveled from Fusa because he was to enter a junior high school, and to any extent that he had problems with anyone on the doctor's homestead, it was not with the maid Inga, he says. There is possibly another explanation. Perhaps the quiet and loyal Inga was irritated by the refractory foster son, but was not about to express this while he was still there.

Bergljot Horne probably said no, perhaps because both she and her son George at the time had serious health problems, but her answer is not filed in the archives.

However Agnes Normann replied with a positive response from Nordfjordeid. On February 11 she wrote:

> Having received your letter to Arne Normann regarding the Jewish boy Edgar Brichta. While he's not currently at home, I sent him the letter and wait for his imminent letter back. I think for sure that this can be done, as both my husband and I myself would like to help him as much as we can. The best solution I think would be to get him into some form of apprenticeship as he did not care to read, and it probably would not be good for him to have nothing to do.
>
> As I certainly believe that this can be arranged I promise to report to you as soon as possible.

Agnes quickly got a response from her husband. Arne Normann who at the time was serving time for treason in custody and preventive detention in Ilebu (today Ila) prison. He had probably received signs that his release on probation was not far off. He would gladly accept Edgar back. This enabled Agnes already on February 19th to give the Jewish Social Committee the confirmation:

> I do hereby inform you that we are willing to take care of our former foster son, Edgar Brichta. Assuming that the travel expenses for his journey to Norway will be covered by by some institution or aid. If this is not the case please notify me as soon as possible.

It is doubtful whether the Jewish organization in Oslo realized, less than three years after the Second World War, that it was about to send Edgar back to a Nazi leader who had been sentenced for treason.

When he answered the letter from Arild Birkeli, Edgar was hardly aware that he would soon move back to Norway, and he had not been in Žilina after the war. Yet he was clearly aware of what he thought had happened to the family, for whom Arild had extended his greetings. In another letter from Nygårdsvik, dated 29 February 1948, his friend was full of remorse:

> I was greatly moved to hear the fate of your parents and sister. I'm sorry I showed so little sensitivity in writing what must have caused a wound to be ripped open.

At this time, Edgar was still taken up with Zionism. He had in fact recommended for Arild to read Arthur Koestler's book of 1946 *Thief in the Night* about the Jewish- Arab dispute over Palestine. Arild replied that he had read a review, and he would follow the recommendation.

But immediately after this, Edgar via AJDC in Bratislava was told that Agnes and Arne wanted him back. Glad to finally have the prospect of a more stable life again after two years of chaos on the continent, he said goodbye to his more radical friends in Hashomer Hatzair. But he had one project before he could leave the country; to visit Žilina. He was enough of a realist, and had largely accepted the probability that his parents were dead, but he would like to know for sure. Besides, he had not given up hope that Vera could be alive.

The central square in Žilina is named after Andrej Hlinka, the man who started the Slovak People's Party and allowed its fascist bands to harass Jews before and during the war. Hlinka is seen today as a sort of founder of Slovakia.

When Edgar in the early spring of 1948 finally came back to his grandmother's old house in search of traces of his family, he at first found nothing. His grandmother's house, where he had lived with his family for a few months in 1939, was there but was occupied by people he had never heard of. He met no one he knew. People he asked at random said they knew nothing.

After a couple of days Edgar nevertheless stumbled upon an older man who knew the Brichtas. It turned out that he had been a friend of his parents, and he remembered the family as it was before the war broke out. Ludevit Donath, as he was named, remembered that his mother Rea and sister Vera had been put on a train in 1942, but he did not know where the train was going and did not know what had happened to the father, Max. At home Mr. Donath had a copy of the book Edgar's father had written and self published. Edgar could not remember having seen it before, but he eagerly and gratefully accepted it as a gift.

Donath also remembered that Edgar's mother just before the outbreak of the war had turned in a pile of bedding to a local laundry, and asked the operator to take care of it until after the war. The same lady still ran the laundry, but denied that Rea Brichta's bedding had been entrusted to her safekeeping. Mr. L. Donath also went with Edgar to the grandmother's house. It was occupied by Slovak families, unknown to either Edgar or Mr. Donath. They did not look happy seeing the two visitors. A potential heir could at worst mean that they had to leave the apartment or pay damages. Edgar was given a brief glimpse of the premises. He saw nothing he could recognize. When they left from there, Ludevit Donath told him the meaning of the Latin phrase *In Vino Veritas*. Donath felt certain that if the present residents had been forthcoming, they could have been able to tell what had happened to Max, Rea and Vera. Getting the current residents under the influence of enough alcohol might lead to revelations of interest. A potential heir could conceivably lead to a request for vacating the premises, or to pay compensation. The only gain for Edgar was his learning a poignant Latin adage.

Edgar opted to move on. His family's fate remained unknown. He more than suspected what had happened. Reluctantly he gave up on further attempts to find his family or to get some documentation of their disappearance. He now had to focus on continuing his life with very little, or no, hope of seeing all the paperwork that was needed to leave. He began to hurry, although Edgar could absolutely not have known it, Czechoslovakia was about to become a communist dictatorship with a flying ban. The Communist Party won the elections in May 1946 with 38 percent of the vote, the best result any communist party in the world had achieved in a free election. Thus, Klement Gottwald became the prime minister. From February 1948 the Communists pushed, with the Soviet Union in the back, in order to take power of the country on a permanent basis. They succeeded in the early summer, and Gottwald became the country's president in June. But then Edgar Brichta - during these last few months in a room rented by the caretaker's wife in her old block in Bratislava -got his papers in order.

Chapter 10

After having been held in custody since May, Arne Normann was interrogated by a police officer at the Division investigating treason cases at the Bergen Police Department in November 1945. The statement is dated 23 November, but must have been obtained over several days.

On 18 closely typed pages Arne explained his actions as a member of the NS (National Unity) and The Hirden [a paramilitary organization during the occupation of Norway by Nazi Germany], as commissioned mayor of the Laksevåg municipality and in his other positions of power. He also responded to a number of accusations for acting as an informer. In a section of the interview called "Subjective factors", he gave the reasons for his initially joining the fight against the German invaders, later going into the NS and becoming a supporter of the occupying power. During the interrogation Arne Normann had mostly used a somber choice of words, he showed no apparent remorse and confirmed many of the conditions of which he was specifically accused. He added that he occasionally aided Laksevåg residents when they got in trouble with the German authorities, but mentioned few or no mitigating circumstances in the usual sense. He said nothing, for example, about Edgar living with him and Agnes during most of the war.

But when a day or two later he came to sign the printed report, he asked to make three additions. The first one dealt with his early1941 approach of the Minister President Vidkun Quisling to ask him to prevent the Germans constructing a submarine base at Damsgårdssundet. This base was reportedly the target of the Allied bombing raid of Bergen in 1944. Arne's last addition dealt with the food Agnes and he had delivered to the Russian prisoners of war in Nygårdssvik. The middle addition reads:

> I might also point out that in 1939 after the outbreak of war I accepted a Jewish refugee boy from Slovakia. He has been in my home during the war.

Probably Arne had talked about the interrogation with other prisoners in The Bergen District Prison where he was during this period. He could have been advised to mention Edgar with the thought that it might lead to getting a lower sentence. That the information about Edgar came as such an addition at least is suggestive that Arne had not been thinking that hiding a Jewish refugee during the war would be beneficial to him in a settlement after the war.

The actual trial did not come up for Bergen County Court until May 19, 1947. The deliberations lasted two days, with the judgment following on the third. The tone of the newspaper report was as it used to be in treason cases after the war, and it was given a lot of space, especially the first day. *Bergens Tidende* presented the defendant and the case this way on May 19:

> A sizable Nazi at the court
>
> Normann, "mayor", "director", etc. has a serious and extensive list of wrongdoings

The hearing in Bergen Arbeiderblad (Bergen Labor paper) the same day was on target:

> "Mayor" Normann is responsible for many things. From minor accusations to wasteful squandering of money

And the Christian newspaper Dagen (The Day):

> "Mayor" Normann in Laksevåg was an informer in grand style

The media coverage followed a clear pattern. The newspapers started by quoting all of the accusations, without clarifying that that was what they were doing. The State Attorney's charges were thus presented as the actual occurrences. This episode - here from *Bergens Tidende*, was reprinted with minor variations in all the papers:

> On August the 2nd, 1942 the accused seized N.N. (authors choice of anonymity) who was in the act of tearing down a legionnaire poster. Normann got the man arrested, gave N.N. several punches with his fists to the face, and during interrogation NN had to suffer serious abuse.

The trial exonerated Normann. He had not hit N.N., it had been done by someone else. The denunciation was nevertheless serious. The detained N.N. was brought to, and then abused vigorously by, the German Gestapo.

The next day, May 20, *Bergens Tidende's* headline read:

> Judgment of six years hard labor for Normann

In a new, lengthy article this was reported from the court proceedings. The prosecutor was thoroughly quoted in the columns. He emphasized that Normann's denunciations were of the "meanest sort", and that he appeared "aggressive" when terminating employees of the municipality of Laksevåg:

> In his total behavior Normann has been so ruthless that no one has exceeded him in my entire practice", the prosecutor emphasized. In favor of the accused, he did say that" after liberation (cessation of war) he has behaved honestly and candidly.

In *The Morgen Avisen* [Morning Newspaper], sarcasm ruled under the title "Nazi mayor of Laksevåg took his duties seriously":

> From the prosecutor's presentation of the case it appears that the accused was a specially dedicated NS man and informer. He pried into everything and if he found something he would run straight to the police. If the Norwegian police were not eager enough, he looked to it that the Germans were notified.

The Morgenavisen added that Arne Normann accepted some self-criticism on this point.

> He admitted to the court that in reality these kinds of issues were for the police to handle and he had no business to get involved in it.

All Bergen newspapers mentioned that Arne Normann had a defender, but no one wrote a word of what the defender might have said in the city court. That the defendant had had a Jewish refugee child living with him during the war, and thus probably saved his life, was hardly mentioned during the proceedings. In any case, nothing is written about Edgar, neither in the newspapers nor in the verdict of the court. But the defendant himself was able to state in the paper *Bergens Tidende* on May 20 without his words being colored by the journalist:

> With regard to joining NS, this happened because he had seen it as his duty to reclaim Norway's freedom and independence, which could happen exclusively through NS. He did not have the feeling that our country was at war with Germany; the opposition was both mostly symbolic and on the whole the collaboration between NS and the Germans was no more extensive than permitted by international law.

The verdict was based on most of the prosecution's charges and assessments, but Arne Normann would still be acquitted of some issues. He got five and a half years of hard labor, six months less than requested by the prosecutor. As usual of those convicted of treason, Arne lost several civil rights for a period of time, including the right to vote and to work in the profession he was trained for. But Arne was excused among other things from confiscation of large sums of money - as had been requested by the prosecution - for his misusing Laksevåg municipality money. In all of the Bergen newspapers, the judgment was rendered in short notices. Three of the four local newspapers emphasized those charges for which Arne Normann acquitted.

The verdict was among the most severe of the treason settlement. In all, about 93,000 Norwegians were investigated, and 50,000 punished. Of those punished, more than 20,000 were imprisoned and 45 got the death penalty.

Arne Normann was given credit for about two years he had spent in custody awaiting his trial. At first he performed convict labor at sundry prison facilities in the Bergen area. Then, from December 12, 1947 he was at Ilebu in Bærum. He was released on parole in July 1948.

Edgar came back to Norway the following month. This time he headed north to Oslo by train, but via Warsaw. Edgar even had to pay for his journey, and it was not simple. He had in fact had to give up his money and other assets to the Zionist organization in Bratislava. Now it was necessary to scrape together a little here and a little there. Again Ludevit Donath provided help. He said he knew that Edgar's father had asked a firm in Bratislava to keep a printing press and some other equipment for him. Edgar visited the company. They acknowledged having some equipment of Max Brichta, and issued a check for Edgar.

Eventually Edgar obtained enough money for a train ticket to Norway. He even had some money left over. This he used to buy presents for Agnes, Arne and Anne, and to Bergljot and her family.

From the Norwegian capital, Edgar took the Bergen line, just as in 1939, but now he got off at Flå station in Hallingdal. He stepped out of the train with a backpack and a map, and started asking people for directions to Slåttemyrsetra, where he would meet Arne, Agnes and Anne.

It was evening, but was still quite light and warm. Edgar wanted to reach the cabin before nightfall. Originally the cabin had been built for use by dairy maids looking after cattle in their summer mountain pastures. A man overheard Edgar's inquiry and came over. The man could tell him that Slåttemyrsetra lay farther up the valley, and that Edgar could not manage to get there before it got dark. Going to the mountains in the dark would be dangerous for someone who was not a local. Einar Føyn, as the man was called, offered Edgar to stay with him in the boarding house where he was staying. He also promised to guide him up to the trail the next day.

Edgar agreed. They ate together that night, and became better acquainted. Føyn was an engineer, lived in Nesøya near Oslo, and was in Flå commissioned by Telecom to plan a new high voltage power line in Hallingdal. He listened carefully to Edgar's story and his plans for the future. Edgar probably also told of Arne Normann and his travails. Quickly Føyn suggested that Edgar could stay with him on Nesøya outside Oslo, while completing his last year of secondary school. It would be more convenient than staying at Arne's, as his situation would be now. Edgar thanked him and thought it sounded like a good idea, but on the condition that Arne and Agnes agreed.

Here it was again: A random meeting with a stranger, making contact, became interested and offered to help. Edgar was still a very young man, and appeared even younger. He must have radiated a powerful charisma.

The following day, Føyn took Edgar to the place where the trail went up to Slåttemyrsetra. Einar Føyn went back to Flå to work, while Edgar set off up the mountain. He arrived in the early afternoon and was greeted by Agnes and Arne. The joy of reunion was great. Adoptive sister, Anne, was there too, but she was still small and did not remember Edgar from before. They were on the mountain because Arne now had a temporary job there as a logger. As a result of the treason sentence, he could not yet work in his old profession as an engineer, and he had to take what he could get.

Arne and Agnes quickly learned about Einar Føyn's offer and they agreed that it would be advantageous for Edgar to stay on Nesøya while he finished secondary school. First, however, he was to spend the remainder of the summer with them in the mountains at the deactivated dairy cabin.

They had much to tell each other, but main topic that evening dealt with the returning foster son's hectic years in his home country. No one was in the mood to talk about the judgment for treason and the ensuing prison time recently terminated. Edgar never brought up that topic, and even Arne touched on it infrequently. Was it shame? We do not know, but it was definitely not a topic of conversation. Edgar recalls that Arne brought up his NS past only on two occasions. Once he made a comment about the treason settlement, specifically the death sentences Vidkun Quisling and other NS leaders had received. Arne disapproved of the government in exile in London having reinstated the death penalty. It was a retroactive law which he found to be: "Disgraceful and un-Norwegian".

Another time Arne told a story from his internment at Ilebu. A group of inmates had decided to try to escape. They began to eat grass and other plants to accustom their body to be able to survive periods when ordinary food would not be available. They were preparing to have to go through fields and forests, without being able to find other food.

Edgar was in Slåttemyrsetra for barely two months. He helped Arne in the forest felling and de-branching trees. A hole was drilled in one end of each log for towing.

The length of each log and the diameter at its mid point was measured and recorded in log books. After the winter snowfall horses would be used to pull the logs down to the valley. Agnes watched Anne, and maintained the household under primitive conditions. The cabin they lived in had no running water or electricity. Water was obtained from a nearby brook. Agnes cooked on a wood burning stove. Kerosene lamps provided light at night. The toilet was a plank across a ditch. Their hair grew long and shaggy on all four. One night Edgar woke as something rummaged in his hair. "What is that?" he asked, a little startled. Arne came with a flashlight, and the light made a mouse jump out of Edgar's hair. He fell asleep at once, but the story was a source of laughter between them for years.

In late September Edgar went to Nesøya to live with Einar Føyn and his family. Einar had arranged admission in Stabekk Municipal Higher public school, so Edgar could now take the final year of secondary school. Life with Einar and Tullik Føyn was nice, and Edgar was thriving at the school. Along with a new friend, Ulf, he frequently went on long bicycle trips, and also on foot or ski. He kept in touch with Bergljot, and Agnes and Arne also by phone.

A letter Arne sent 20 November is preserved. At this time he had worked for three weeks as a machinist in a Government-owned power station for a fish fillet processing and cold storage facility in Melbu, in his home municipality of Hadsel. Arne said in the letter, he lived in a single room, but went home to Stokmarknes on weekends.

> It has now been 1.5 months since we parted there in Flå. How time goes fast, too fast. I hear from Agnes that you are doing well, and that makes me feel happy. You were not a big guy when you came to us in 1939 and it is strange that you have become like family in a way.

Arne wrote that he was struggling to find a permanent job. He would like to start a business of his own. Among other things, he had tried to obtain machinery for flatbread production, without success. But he stressed that his health and spirit were good. Soon Agnes and Anne will come up for Christmas with *Hurtigruta* [a coastal passenger ship]:

> Poor them, they are both so miserable at sea. They will probably look green when they arrive.

Arne enclosed a picture of himself, as well as a ten crown note. He asked Edgar to write soon and tell what was happening at school and elsewhere.

Edgar wrote back, but believing that Arne now struggled more than he, Edgar, did – as Arne had wife and daughter to look after - so he sent the ten crown back. Arne sounded almost annoyed when in another letter of December 15:

> But that you would send back the 10 crown! You were welcome to use them. A boy of your age can always use money. It was just so little. I tried together with Sivert - you know he has good black market connections - to obtain a windbreaker for you, but unfortunately the one we got was not of a suitable size.

Arne sent 20 crown back south with a clear message: "Do not hurt me by returning them." The tone of the letter was otherwise quite depressed, although Arne stressed that he was treated well by the people of his home community. That was more than could have been expected for those who had been convicted of treason. Arne still had his temporary job as a machinist at the local power plant, but he was applying for jobs in the south of Norway, at the time without a bite. He had also been unable to find a permanent residence for himself and his family. Living quarters were generally in short supply in Norway during the years after the war. Those punished for treason had no priority if others were seeking rentals. Agnes and Anne had to remain living with her family in Nordfjordeid. Arne took, he wrote, "a step at a time, so we'll see how things turn out".

> Life has not shown itself in the best light for you, yet in the final view it may not matter. One can in any case find that life is interesting.

The foster father - formally he was that, although now Edgar lived with another - hoped to meet again soon:

> I would like to keep a hand on you (on your ear!), you know, and I have now found some decent work and an apartment, so everything has improved.

In his letter Edgar had obviously aired the idea of going to sea, and Arne commented on this:

> We will discuss your plans to go to sea later. Agnes said you would be an outstanding restaurateur (that is a gourmand).

The letters between Nesøya and Melbu came close together during this period. Edgar replied before Christmas in a letter attached to Christmas gifts. Arne acknowledged receiving them with a letter January 1, 1949. He thanked him for "a nice cigarette case". Although the weather was "incredibly bad", Arne's mood had taken an upturn. The reason was that he had obtained a new job of which he seemed proud. Monday Arne would start as a plant engineer of a workshop in Bogen, Ofoten. This was somewhat surprising since two years earlier he was deprived of his right to work in the profession he was trained for, i.e. as an engineer. Maybe the position was not formally designated as an engineering position, but as something more neutral, such as "operations manager".

Anyway, this did not pass unnoticed, and the story was told to Anne by her father many years later: Initially Arne did not report his treason sentence when he applied for jobs. He wanted to avoid being excluded at the outset, and assumed that the business administrators who were interested in applicants' NS past, would do their own checking. For the application for the job in Bogen, he had therefore not mentioned anything about his sentence.

But when Arne was prepared to start the job, a board member of the union at the workshop found out about Arne's NS past. The Union

Board considered the matter and decided to put it up for a vote by the union members. At the meeting, the discussion was heated. If all union members were to accept Arne Normann as a colleague, the management would support employment. If someone voted against it, the Union would do everything to prevent him from getting hired. Voting results showed that all but one voted yes to accept Arne. The majority found it was too bad that this one, a young guy, would be able to block Arne's acceptance. They put pressure on the man, who finally caved, and things went well. For Arne, this event was a psychological turning point, and since then, he told Anne, he always told would-be employers about his sentence when he applied for a job.

Whether the drama of the union took place before or after this letter to Edgar is uncertain. Probably it came afterwards. In any case Arne, in his letter to Edgar, could inform him that in the last two weeks he had received the Slovak newspaper *Pravda* [Truth], addressed to Edgar. What should he do with the newspaper? Edgar doesn't recall today that he had ever subscribed to the newspaper, nor who may have paid for it.

Of greater interest is a passage in the letter in which Arne commented on something Edgar had written about a person he had contact with in Eastern Norway.

> You have your difficulties to contend with also, I understand from your letter. You do not think that NN (will remain anonymous) is particularly excited about the Jews. Oh no, it might be so, I do not know. In this country, we are very smug, it cannot be denied, but we have no bitterness against the Jews; I think even now that is so. Before the war, there was in any case no Jewish hatred here. Yes, even during the war, among the ordinary NS members there were very few who were actually hateful, I think. But now it may be possible that such sentiments, secondary to English influence, as usual gently and almost imperceptibly, may guide the opinion about Jews into other paths than before. We shall see. Today, anything is possible.

Arne was not sympathetic to the Norwegian authorities after the war and mentioned in the letter that he believes that they did both wiretapping and spying on the mail - "you should not write too much".

> ...we'll leave behind each day's troubles, but also be ready to act resolutely and powerfully if conditions indicate it's necessary.

Towards the end of the letter he went back to the private:

> When you finish school this summer and you probably decide to come to us, then we'll see. However, I wish you, dear Edgar, well in 1949 and thank you for the good times we had together.

Edgar completed his school in at Stabekk Community Higher School with flying colors. On the recommendation of his teachers he was awarded the nation's award for the year 1948/49 issued to exceptionally gifted youth. He received 200 crown as well as a ticket for the National Theater to see the performance of Henrik Ibsen's 'The Wild Duck'. Judging from the preserved letters, he was in touch with Agnes and Arne Normann at this time more than with Bergljot Horne and the others. Edgar sent Agnes and Arne packages with things they could not so easily get in northern Norway at this time. In a package he sent Agnes winter boots and yarn. She thought it was wrong that Edgar sent her his boots, so returned them. But Agnes happily thanked him and welcomed the yarn. She responded by knitting earmuffs for Edgar, which she, for lack of a pattern, had to knit using her imagination. Arne and Agnes sent him small sums of money now and then. Life in Bogen i Ofoten was not particularly attractive, even though Arne did well at his job. "Of friends and diversions, there are none", Agnes writes in a letter April 16, 1949.

Edgar still lacked two points to graduate with the highest grades overall. Later he regretted that while he was taking the German exam, he had tried to impress the commission with a wording that he thought was more authentic than the one chosen by the examiners.

The last few months of high school, Edgar pondered on what he should do next. As he failed to get a visa to the U.S., he had to consider other approaches. Remaining in Norway was a possibility. He felt increasingly Norwegian, and with a good secondary school exam, he had a good foundation for further study. Arne checked the possibilities of getting him a job as a gardener. He knew of a firm in Molde where he might find a spot for Edgar. Agnes still wrote in her letters that he should become a chef since he was good at cooking.

The summer of 1949 went by fast. Edgar worked at doing odds and ends at the office of the Nig large photo equipment company. Nights he spent in a cabin, free of rent, on Næsøya. The cabin belonged to the Føyns. When he was not at work Edgar visited friends, Ulf Güssow and Kirsten Eggum, his former schoolmates. Weekends he took bicycle trips with his friends.

His relatives in both Canada and the USA urged him to come to the New World. Deliberating with mixed emotions, Edgar decided to keep his option to remain in Norway, but also to visit any remaining relatives he could locate. As his earnings would not enable him to take excursions to America and he was not about to ask to be subsidized, he decided to get a job as a sailor. Einar was again helpful as he found a ships broker in need of a budding seaman.

The *S/S Livia*, a cargo ship plying the seas carrying freight between ports wherever needed [as opposed to traveling between certain ports].

Edgar told Arne and Agnes about his plans, and got a reply on June 14:

> As we are to understand, you've already been hired, and it might not be a bad idea.

The tone of the letter is lighter, maybe because the weather also was better. Agnes complained that Arne had so much to do, also at home in the evenings:

> I get upset every time I see him bring in that pile of work so that I am often tempted to give him a thrashing, and so help me, I am afraid that I will assault him one fine day.

Agnes urged Edgar to take a trip to Nordfjordeid now that school was finished. Maybe he could borrow a bicycle from Føyn and pedal through Gudbrandsdalen via Grotli and Videsæter and on to Eid? She thought it would be a great trip.

> If there would be a day when you were not in a mood to ride your bike you could just take the bus. But to sit and suffer in these crowded and smelly buses is not fun at all.

Soon after Arne also sent a letter in which he said that his father was now dead, and the last family members were planning to move from Stokmarknes, "so that period of life is over". Arne also sent 100 crowns for travel money and wished Edgar good luck on the seven seas:

> When you now travel, dear Edgar, I wish you well for your future. If it happens that we can meet again, you are always welcome to stay with us. There will always be a vacant spot for you with us. I hope we will hear from you now and then.

In the letter Arne complained that Edgar did not take the trip to Nordfjordeid before he signed on, but there he was wrong. Exactly at this time, Edgar sat on the bike and pedaled all across the mountain. The brakes began to smoke on the steep downward slope toward the Nordfjord. He spent a few summer weeks with the Sætre family. Even Agnes and Anne came down from northern Norway to visit with him, but Arne had to stay overseeing his work.

Chapter 11

EDGAR AND A SECOND mate who also signed on to *SS Livia* travelled together from Oslo to Genoa. There the ship was unloading peanuts from the U.S. Since Edgar knew peanuts and liked them, he happily grabbed a handful. Now he learned that raw peanuts do not taste good.

SS Livia was a so-called Liberty Ship, mass produced in the United States during World War II, mostly to replace losses in the British Merchant Navy. Although the ship had just arrived from the U.S., Edgar had no guarantee that it would bring him back to America, even if this was what he was hoping for.

Liberty ships were welded together instead of rivetted, which shortened the production time. This made the Liberty ships somewhat controversial among sailors. Established sailors on board told the newly arrived cabin boy that ships like these often broke and sank in heavy seas. Edgar was not intimidated by that. On board, his job was to bring food and drinks from the galley to the officers' mess hall, serving the food, and later clearing the tables, washing dishes and, keeping the area clean and tidy. As a rookie, he started at the bottom of the ship pecking order, and got told off by some of the officers, sometimes with good reason. Eventually, he gained supporters. Once, the chief cook arrived back from shore leave overly drunk. He came to the officers' mess hall and vomited copiously. Edgar got to clean it up. For ever after the head cook was generous and helpful towards Edgar. Another ally of Edgar was Niko Elman, a Dutch able-bodied seaman. Niko asked for and got lessons in mathematics from Edgar who in turn got to refresh the subject he had learnt in school.

After visiting some other ports, *SS Livia* got a load bound for Philadelphia on the U.S. east coast.

One day as he was working in the officers' mess hall, Edgar heard the first mate tell about how pleased he was that a sailor who recently had deserted the ship, had sense enough to take all his belongings. It saved the first mate from having to rummage through dirty socks and other belongings, catalog the lot and send it to the company home office.

Another time an experienced sailor was telling of an American war time rule. Able bodied men who entered the USA without authorization could enter the armed forces and after serving time in the military could apply for, and be granted, legal residence.

Edgar's plan was hatched.

The evening after *SS Livia* had docked at pier 46N in Philadelphia, Edgar with his modestly sized suitcase quietly walked down the gangplank. He found his way to the railroad station and placed his suitcase in a locker. He went back on board. Early in the morning the day *S/S Livia* was slated to leave, he left for the railroad station. The train for New York was departing at 6.15 AM. By 8:40 AM he was in New York.

He had an envelope with an address on it which he showed to a taxi driver. The driver efficiently found the Manhattan address. Edgar had seen the taximeter and was happy that the figure was well below the $5.00 note he had which he handed over to the driver. The latter gave Edgar a heavy handful of coins and departed. Later Edgar added up the value of the coins and discovered it was but a minor fraction of what was due him. He realized that he had much to learn about life in the New World. The address he had reached was of a grocery store operated by Hungarian immigrants. Its clientele included many newcomers to New York. Edgar's aunt, Gisela Spitzer and Eduard Wolf, the father of her husband had, used the grocery store's services in preparing and sending packages to Edgar. They consisted of clothing and easy to send food items.

Edgar ended up with Eduard Wolf, an elderly man living alone in a one room apartment. Edgar got to sleep on the floor there the first few days. He remembers the old man best for his breakfast: half a grapefruit with a jigger of whiskey poured over it. Within a day Mr. Eduard W. took Edgar with him to an acquaintance of his, a Slovakian Jew who had participated in the armed struggle against the Germans. Mr. Jakubovič made a living mostly by importing and exporting various commodities. Most of his customers were other immigrants, often in need of having documents translated, or having forms filled out and having letters written. This man, Herman Jakubovič helped Edgar find a furnished room to rent in the Bronx. Edgar paid $4.50 a week rent. He found work as a messenger where he was earning 90 cents per hour. Within weeks of his arrival the first minimum wage regulation was inaugurated in New York. His wages jumped to $1.00 per hour. He started attending evening high school.

Since Edgar was illegally in the U.S., he assumed an alias 'Bernard Levin'. He used his real name, however, when he signed up for the Selective Service, the agency in which all males past 18 years of age had to register.

While working as a messenger and office helper he was given an opportunity to learn various forms of reproducing printed forms. This included mimeographing, multi graphing and offset printing. He also had to tidy up and clean up the work spaces, deliver completed work to customers, and once a week go to the bank for the funds for the weekly pay roll of the five or six employees. Edgar planned to obtain a residence permit just by going into the armed forces. He made new friends, and they went out together a few times to whatever the Metropolis had to offer. Once crossing Times Square along with three friends from school he was hailed by a youth. It did not take long to recognize Alan from the days in the Slovakian Zionist residence in Bratislava. Alan had come to the USA with his mother and sister. Alan invited Edgar to meet his mother and sister. Edgar was introduced to the sister, Judy Lahr. She had survived the war with forged identification and by being hidden in sundry, mostly rural areas of the country. Her circumstances were turbulent and precarious, as dramatic as those experienced by Edgar. Thus, they had much to talk about, while interest developed into love.

A letter from Bergljot Horne, postmarked November 29, 1949, tells its own story. Or rather, the envelope does. Bergljot sent it to Edgar Brichta with address '*SS Livia* company Simonsen / Astrup, Fr. Nansen Square 9, Oslo'. The company obviously did not know where Edgar now was, and returned the letter to Bergljot, with an inscription on the front of the envelope. "Addressee deserted ship while "Livia" left Phil., PA, 11/12/48". On the back was "Brichta paycheck for November was stopped. When contacting our office a settlement will be prepared". Bergljot sent the letter to the address of a relative of Edgar's in New York. Apparently they had moved but the letter was forwarded to a current address. It reached him in the end. Bergljot mentioned again about her health problem, but said she had recovered.

> I thought so of you, Edgar - where in the world are you right now? Suddenly I look at the globe and think: Where in the world is Edgar peregrinating? And then I think that I will go straight away and write to you, but then comes a phone call or something and it gets postponed.

It turned out that Bergljot and Edgar corresponded somewhat in 1949, although this letter is the only one that has survived. In a previous letter she had told him that she bought lottery tickets where the main prize was a radio, which Edgar would get if she won. Now the drawing had taken place:

> Do you know who won the radio? A German brat! I cried that evening, I was so bitter. I had a firm notion in my head that I should win it - I had got tickets for 27 crown in your name - but no!

She also recalled when Edgar took a short trip to Bergen to visit her about a year before: "I'll never forget how handsome you were when you were standing there in the doorway!!"

Edgar moved in with Judy and her family in the Bronx. After a while, he and Judy's brother decided to look for work in San Francisco. While he was on the west coast, the Selective Service System summoned him to take the compulsory physical and psychological tests. Not long after came the call to active duty. Edgar traveled back to New York. He visited Judy elated with his progress. Then he went to the U.S. immigration authorities on Columbus Circle in New York. With the draft notice in hand, Edgar confidently entered the immigration and naturalization office building. The secretary sent him up to the sixth floor for further processing. He was surprised when he realized he had landed in the investigation and enforcement division of the immigration and naturalization department. Two sympathetic agents explained how after the capitulation of Japan, the law exempting foreign men from the entry visa requirement had changed. Previously, with the conditions that they were able bodied and willing to serve in the military, and a congress member entered their name on a list to defer the usual visa requirement, foreign men could apply for and be granted legal residence. Edgar remembers that the agents were almost as unhappy as he himself with the new rules.

He had to spend the night in a police holding cell. The next morning Edgar was transported to Ellis Island where the U.S. detained illegal immigrants. Through the barbed wire fence, he had a panoramic view of the Statue of Liberty's rear.

After ten days he was released on bail raised by his relatives. He was given a clear message from the government: Edgar had 30 days to leave the U.S. voluntarily. If he was on time and went out of the country on his own, he could apply for a reentry permit in the future. If not, the family would lose the bail money, and he would be sent to the country he came from with the U.S. footing the bill. Then the right to apply for entry would be denied forever.

Edgar realized he had only one thing to do. At the Norwegian Seamen's office he found a ship, *M/S Tancred* in need of an engine boy. In March 1952, Edgar signed on this ship owned by Wilh. Wilhelmsen's shipping company. The voyage led through the Panama Canal, on to San Francisco, and finally to Japan, Hong Kong the Philippines (Cebu, Zambuanga, Manila). Then back to the USA, where he signed off, for a short visit to Judy before taking a job on a tanker ship, the *M/T Sirocco.* It brought him as close to Palestine as he ever got. The Sirocco was taking on a load of crude oil from Sidon, Lebanon and Edgar had hoped to get a day off to visit nearby Israel. For the filling of the holds, the ship was anchored in the bay a safe distance from shore while the oil was pumped on board through massive hoses. No shore leaves were granted unless a crew member had to be seen by a physician or a dentist. To make these ships more desirable for the crew members they received a hazard bonus added to their pay. The *Sirocco* when fully loaded set course for Canada where the oil was transferred to large containers on shore near Montreal. Edgar began to plan for a carrier on land. He decided to return to Norway to make some definitive decisions about his future.

He changed ships, for the last time as a sailor as he became a fire tender on *M/S Blue Master*, owned by the shipping company Golden West in Oslo. After five months at sea, Edgar finally ended up in Narvik in northern Norway. To facilitate his separation from *Blue Master*, Edgar gave the information that he had not yet served his obligatory stint in the Norwegian military.

Thus for the third time Edgar arrived in Norway, and for the third time he was off to Arne and Agnes Normann. Arne now 44 and Agnes 46 years old. Anne was 12. Arne was employed as an engineer at the state owned Årdal and Sunndal Works in Sunndalsøra. He helped Edgar get his clothes and other personal belongings sent over from New York, and also arranged for a job for him at Arne's workplace. Edgar kept at it just for a few months. The work was monotonous, and for a steadily evolving adventurer now 22 years old, it was not likely to lead to much advancement. Sunndalsøra was not a bustling metropolis, and Edgar did not establish any close friendships there. The contact with Arne and Agnes was as it had always been, mostly good. Once, Arne made a stinging remark that expressed a negative view of Jews. Edgar responded by saying that the Jews were now much stronger, and that they would defend themselves better if they were attacked again. Arne had then mumbled something about Jews probably "could still use a good beating".

Early in 1953 Edgar moved to eastern Norway. He lived for a while with a friend, Ulf Güssow and his family, in Slependen before he was offered the use of a cabin belonging to Einar Føyn. It lay on the outer coast, some distance from Føyn's house. Einar Einar managed to secure a position for Edgar. Full of enthusiasm Edgar trotted in to what he perceived to be a career in journalism. It was not. He was shown how to clean the huge inky rollers of the printing presses at given times throughout each day. He walked away disappointed. On his own he found an entry level job at Nærliens, a photography firm in Oslo. At the same time he signed up for evening classes in an evening gymnasium (college).

Maintaining postal contact with his relatives and with the immigration agencies in the USA and Canada he began to focus on the need of preparing for a suitable career. He also stayed in touch with Agnes, Arne and Bergljot. Agnes said in a letter of July 17, 1953 that the three had been blueberry picking, and she had been bitten by insects, with the result that "one of my pretty legs looks like a log". Later that autumn, Edgar excitedly wrote that he was finally approved for an entry visa *Over There*, more specifically to Canada, with the help of relatives. This time Arne responded. He expanded on the nice autumn to be expected in the country of the Northwest. "But it blows, you know, something like it did when you were on a bike ride up in Lilledalen". A bit

Arne's parents in the 1930's or 40's.

sad, Arne remembered that Edgar did not thrive in Sunndalsøra – "I can understand, in a way" - and he rejoiced that Edgar finally got entry into Canada.

> I do not know your plans, but you are so wise when it comes to making arrangements for yourself. You are young and strong, and with that one can overcome everything. It can however be good to know that if any stressful things arise then you have other options. You can count on us just as if this were your home.

Arne also transmitted greetings and wishes of good luck from Agnes and Anne – "they both sit right now here in the living room with their noses down into knitting and sewing".

November 20, 1953 Edgar Brichta went aboard *the SS Stavangerfjord*, also known as the 'Queen of the Atlantic Ocean'. This time he was a paying passenger. An attempt to find a ship that would let Edgar work on board for his passage fell through. The trip went from Oslo to New York. Edgar spent a few days there with Judy and her family, before he took the train to Montreal. There he stayed with a family befriended by Edgar's relatives in New York. After he found a rental place Judy came to Montreal. They were married in Montreal on April 19, 1954. Eventually they would have five children together. The third, the first girl, was called Agnes.

In 1954, Edgar also went into the office of the Christian youth organization YMCA in Montreal to register for a course in their school, Sir George Williams College. The secretary assisting him with the required paper work was of Danish origin and married to a Norwegian man from Trondheim. Mrs. Brodahl, the secretary, not only helped with Edgar's enrollment at the school she also talked to the administrators about Edgar's experience with printing machines. Edgar was hired as the college printer for which he was paid a modest salary and also received free tuition.

Once again Edgar was fortunate in meeting people who would help him along. Sir George Williams Collage had an agreement with McGill University, located just up the hill above Sir George Williams College. Each year, one qualified applicant out of the graduating class from SGWC wishing to study medicine at McGill University would be admitted. In 1957 this became Edgar. Judy found employment as a secretary. Edgar earned a little by working evenings as a chemistry laboratory assistant at SGWC. Additional support came from a local organization of physicians' wives in Montreal, and from Edgar's relatives in New York.

Thus Edgar Brichta was educated to become a physician. He received his medical degree on May 1, 1961. At that time Judy and Edgar had two sons and one daughter. The most family friendly training hospital Edgar visited was Saint Benedict's Hospital in Ogden, Utah. There Edgar completed a rotating internship and Judy delivered their third son, Paul. As Edgar had shared with another graduate the highest standing in pediatrics of the class of 1961, he was persuaded by the attending pediatricians of Saint Benedicts' to pursue pediatric specialty training at the Washington University Affiliated Hospitals in Seattle, WA, where their fifth and final child was born.

After additional training in Maternal and Child Health (at UC Berkeley) and a psychiatry residency at the Institute of Living in Hartford, Connecticut, he worked as a psychiatrist in California and for seven years in the U.S. Air Force.

While serving at the Ramstein Air Base near Kaiserslautern in then West Germany from 1974 to 1977, Judy, Edgar and the children went to Norway to visit Tullik and Einar Føyn on the coast near Oslo, and Agnes and Arne Normann in Sunndalsøra. Later, three of the children traveled to Norway to visit on their own. Judy and Edgar went to Europe in 1992. First, they went to Czechoslovakia, where they tried to get to the bottom of what had happened to his family. In Bratislava, it was not possible to find out anything. The most important archives were still closed.

In Žilina, they found the grandmother's house in ruins behind a barrier. It had been demolished by the municipality just a few days before they arrived. Edgar had a thought that his mother, if she suddenly had to flee the house, could have hidden something in the basement. But now only piles of bricks mortar and lumber remained behind a temporary fence. It was Friday only hours before the scheduled departure for Český Těšín. There they went to the county offices to obtain a printed copy of Vera's birth certificate. The attending office clerk explained that such requests were only issued on certain days of the week, and this unfortunately was a wrong day. Edgar and Judy said they were traveling from the USA, and did not have the opportunity to wait for the next correct day. Could they make an exception? The answer was "no". In the afternoon, Edgar and Judy tried to find the house where the family had lived when Vera was born. Edgar could not remember the address, only that it was near a brick factory. They found the factory, now closed, and all the houses around were abandoned, but he was unable to trace the right house.

The last stop for Judy and Edgar in central Europe was Auschwitz, the vast complex of concentration camps in the town called Oświeçim in

Polish. No official confirmation had been issued. Rumors and sporadic accounts by camp survivors pointed to the probability that Max, Rea and Vera ended their days in 1942. The facility became a war memorial and museum. Visitors can also look at piles of shoes taken from prisoners who were gassed to death. Edgar was looking for small shoes that might have belonged to seven year old Vera. There were many.

Then Judy and Edgar went to Norway. In Sunndalsøra they visited the grave of Agnes Normann. She had died the year before. Arne was still alive, but was in his 85th year and hard hit by Alzheimer's disease. He was neat and well dressed, and had a private room at the nursing home, but was no longer able to communicate in a meaningful way. Strangely enough, he had the best connection with Judy, whom he had met only once before. He even talked in English. Arne Normann died two years later.

It wasn't until the mid-1990s, after the Iron Curtain fell, and a slow process to make old records available, that Edgar Brichta got a fairly clear idea what had happened to his family. The city where they lived, Žilina, was singled out in 1942 as one of three transit camps for Slovakia's Jews. There they were sent, waiting for the transport to Auschwitz, Treblinka, Sobibor and other death camps. On March 26, 1942 the trains began to go. Maximilian, Regina and Vera Brichta were locked up in the Žilina camp April 30, 1942, according to documents held in the Slovak National Archives. A week later, on May 7th, they were' 'released' from the camp. The deportation train to Auschwitz in German-occupied Poland was waiting for them. Upon arrival, there were some Jews taken out to various kinds of work, which extended and in some cases helped to save lives. But Edgar's parents were too old and his sister too young. Probably they were gassed immediately.

In the autumn of 2008, the Holocaust museum sent Edgar Brichta a copy of the receipt for the transport of his parents and sister to Auschwitz in 1942. Nearer to their grave he will never come. In memory of his family Edgar sent a gift to Bill Clinton's presidential library in Little Rock, Arkansas. On cobblestones in the symbolic bridge says "Vera Brichta 1935-1942, Regina Brichta 1901-1942, Maximilian Brichta 1886-1942."

Epilogue

by Edgar Brichta

March 3, 1886
January 31, 1901
January 21, 1935

THESE ARE THE BIRTHDAYS of my father Max, my mother Rea and my sister Vera.

The last time I saw them was in October 1939. Together with 36 other Jewish children from Czechoslovakia, I was then being sent to Norway accompanied by two women. This journey had been arranged so that we, the children, would be removed from the steadily worsening conditions in Central Europe. My parents had never been to Scandinavia. To make the parting easier they spoke with enthusiasm about how kind the Norwegians were, and about the beauty of the country I was headed for - the land where the descendants of Vikings were living and the midnight sun was shining.

My anxiety over having to leave my family and home was calmed by my wish to show that I could manage and by my curiosity about what I would experience. I anticipated ocean, mountains, and kind people, and counted on the war ending before I completed my elementary school requirements. Then I would travel back as a homecoming globetrotter and tell about all I had experienced.

These are memories which have faded with the passing time, suppressed by happenings during seven decades. The arrival in Norway was memorable. My parents had not exaggerated. I met my foster parents, the Nansen Help representatives and the school teachers. All were friendly and accommodating and eagerly commenced teaching me Norwegian.

From my earliest years I readily attached myself to people. I became overjoyed when meeting new people, and quickly became part of everyday life in Nygårdsvik.

Early on the morning of April 9, 1940 my peaceable adjustment got suddenly disturbed by sounds of explosions, gun shots and whining bullets. Outside the window, I saw soldiers crawling with guns aiming towards Kvarven. My foster parents tried every way possible to assure me that we would be safe. I trusted them fully. But I did begin to wonder what might be happening to my family when even peaceable Norway was experiencing this. My optimism was also being challenged when I had to relinquish my newly acquired Boy Scout uniform at the order of the occupying forces. Later on I was informed that our Scout troop leader had been arrested and executed.

At about that time a schoolmate of mine caught diphtheria and died. He had been the only boy in my class as short as I was. His passing weighed heavily on me. His funeral was the first one I attended.

I became most surprised when I discovered that my foster father had joined the NS party (Nazi). He continued to treat me well. I never felt that he would permit any harm to fall upon me. That something was awry I first sensed from my friends.

From the beginning of 1942 I received no more mail from Slovakia. I often wondered how my parents, my sister and my grandmother were managing. I strenuously held on to the belief that I would meet them again. I clung to the thought that the reason I was getting no mail from them was because acts of war interfered with the transportation of the mail. I had sensed that the people in Slovakia were not overly fond of minorities as Gypsies and Jews. Over the radio I had heard speeches by Hitler and Goebels and they sounded accusatory and threatening.

On May10, 1945, right after the armistice with Germany I mailed a letter to my parents. It came returned to me with a message from the Swedish postal service advising me that the letter could not be forwarded as the postal connection to the destination country was disrupted. My hope of a joyful family reunion dwindled. Yet I could not give up on the thought that damages to all means of transportation had been so severely damaged that mail could not move freely.

By and by I did make contact with aunts and uncles in England, Canada and the USA. None of them knew anything about the whereabouts of my parents, sister and grandmother.

On leaving Norway in 1946 I was not optimistic. The tales of death camps and gas chambers gave me a chilling sensation. For the longest I held out the hope that my little sister young, gentle, and in the time I knew her, lively and even tempered would be hidden somewhere by caring people. I focused on my approach to find her.

In 1948 I met a friend of my parents in Žilina. He made it clear that the last trip my family made was in May 1942 and that shortly after leaving the cattle train wagon their lives were no more.

I have read what survivors have described. Repeatedly I have conjured up images of my little sisters demure, hopeful and helpless. Maybe some human being saw her and snatched her from death. Or at least saw her while still alive. If there is anyone who travelled that grizzly train to Auschwitz in May 1942 let me hear from you. My e-mail address is: edgarsb30@juno.com

In the period after the end of the second world war, I was confused about Arne's attachment to the Nazis. I continued to respect him as a good human being who truly wanted to help me survive and have success in my life. His attachment to an organization that promulgated extermination of Jews, Gypsies, mentally impaired people and others considered undesirable created a dilemma for me. Gradually I became convinced that he had not looked in depth into cultural and social issues. Having felt abandoned by the Allied forces in April and May of 1940, he became receptive to German propaganda. This was reinforced by Quisling and Terboven. I think Arne did not know of Germany's extermination camps until after the end of the war. What he may have read or heard during the war could be swept aside as Allied propaganda spread to make Germany look bad.

Agnes was a gentle and good woman. She respected others, was tolerant and had empathy for others, especially those who suffered. She was skeptical about Arne's political views and actions during the war years. She never did express any support for the national socialists. The only time I remember Agnes talk about the occupiers was once when I went with her on the ferry on the way home from Bergen. She told Arne that some of the German soldiers looked so nice and decent that she could understand that Norwegian girls could fall for them.

I maintained contact with Agnes and Arne as long as they lived. They were the best substitute parents I could have wished for. I admire them for all they have done for me.

I am grateful for the conscientious work Bjarte Bruland and Frank Rossavik have dedicated to this book. They have joined the list of benefactors and friends I have found in Norway. Agnes and Arne Normann remain high in my esteem. The same applies to the family of Horne-Maisey, of Kari Øpstad, Aslaug Blytt, the Føyn family and all who aided me in avoiding a premature death. Thank you all for the rewarding life you granted me.

The three birthdates that initiated this epilogue have now been transformed from pertaining to indistinguishable ashes to enshrine dear human beings whose memory is warmly loved.

Sacramento in the spring of 2009,

Edgar Brichta

Edgar Brichta (født 1930) er i dag pensjonert lege og bosatt i Sacramento i California, sammen med sin kone Judy, som også overlevde Holocaust. Han har fem barn og åtte barnebarn. (Foto: Robert Durell)

Edgars far, Max Brichta, drev som tryllekunstner og hypnotisør i 1920-årene. Dette er omslaget til en bok han ga ut i 1930, året da Edgar ble født.